GLORIA NAYLOR

Photo by Sigrid Estrada. Courtesy of Gloria Naylor.

GLORIA NAYLOR

A Critical Companion

Charles E. Wilson, Jr.

CRITICAL COMPANIONS TO POPULAR CONTEMPORARY WRITERS
Kathleen Gregory Klein, Series Editor

Greenwood Press
Westport, Connecticut • London

Library of Congress Cataloging-in-Publication Data

Wilson, Charles E. 1961–
    Gloria Naylor : a critical companion / Charles E. Wilson, Jr.
        p. cm.—(Critical companions to popular contemporary writers, ISSN 1082–4979)
    Includes bibliographical references (p.   ) and index.
    ISBN 0–313–31330–X (alk. paper)
    1. Naylor, Gloria—Criticism and interpretation.   2. Women and literature—United
States—History—20th century.   3. Afro-American women in literature.   4. Afro-
Americans in literature.   I. Title.   II. Series.
PS3564.A895Z97   2001
813'.54—dc21   00–052134

British Library Cataloguing in Publication Data is available.

Library of Congress Catalog Card Number: 00–052134
ISBN: 0–313–31330–X
ISSN: 1082–4979

First published in 2001

Greenwood Press, 88 Post Road West, Westport, CT 06881
An imprint of Greenwood Publishing Group, Inc.
www.greenwood.com

Printed in the United States of America

The paper used in this book complies with the
Permanent Paper Standard issued by the National
Information Standards Organization (Z39.48–1984).

10 9 8 7 6 5 4 3 2 1

For Charles, Sr., and Mattie Hogg Wilson,
my eternal mentors.

Contents

Series Foreword

The authors who appear in the series Critical Companions to Popular Contemporary Writers are all best-selling writers. They do not simply have one successful novel, but a string of them. Fans, critics, and specialist readers eagerly anticipate their next book. For some, high cash advances and breakthrough sales figures are automatic; movie deals often follow. Some writers become household names, recognized by almost everyone.

But, their novels are read one by one. Each reader chooses to start and, more importantly, to finish a book because of what she or he finds there. The real test of a novel is in the satisfaction its readers experience. This series acknowledges the extraordinary involvement of readers and writers in creating a best-seller.

The authors included in this series were chosen by an Advisory Board composed of high school English teachers and high school and public librarians. They ranked a list of best-selling writers according to their popularity among different groups of readers. For the first series, writers in the top-ranked group who had received no book-length, academic, literary analysis (or none in at least the past ten years) were chosen. Because of this selection method, Critical Companions to Popular Contemporary Writers meets a need that is being addressed nowhere else. The success of these volumes as reported by reviewers, librarians, and teachers led to an expansion of the series mandate to include some writers with wide critical attention—Toni Morrison, John Irving, and Maya Angelou, for example—to extend the usefulness of the series.

The volumes in the series are written by scholars with particular expertise in analyzing popular fiction. These specialists add an academic focus to the popular success that these writers already enjoy.

The series is designed to appeal to a wide range of readers. The general reading public will find explanations for the appeal of these well-known writers. Fans will find biographical and fictional questions answered. Students will find literary analysis, discussions of fictional genres, carefully organized introductions to new ways of reading the novels, and bibliographies for additional research. Whether browsing through the book for pleasure or using it for an assignment, readers will find that the most recent novels of the authors are included.

Each volume begins with a biographical chapter drawing on published information, autobiographies or memoirs, prior interviews, and, in some cases, interviews given especially for this series. A chapter on literary history and genres describes how the author's work fits into a larger literary context. The following chapters analyze the writer's most important, most popular, and most recent novels in detail. Each chapter focuses on one or more novels. This approach, suggested by the Advisory Board as the most useful to student research, allows for an in-depth analysis of the writer's fiction. Close and careful readings with numerous examples show readers exactly how the novels work. These chapters are organized around three central elements: plot development (how the story line moves forward), character development (what the reader knows of the important figures), and theme (the significant ideas of the novel). Chapters may also include sections on generic conventions (how the novel is similar or different from others in its same category of science, fantasy, thriller, etc.), narrative point of view (who tells the story and how), symbols and literary language, and historical or social context. Each chapter ends with an "alternative reading" of the novel. The volume concludes with a primary and secondary bibliography, including reviews.

The alternative readings are a unique feature of this series. By demonstrating a particular way of reading each novel, they provide a clear example of how a specific perspective can reveal important aspects of the book. In the alternative reading sections, one contemporary literary theory—way of reading, such as feminist criticism, Marxism, new historicism, deconstruction, or Jungian psychological critique—is defined in brief, easily comprehensible language. That definition is then applied to the novel to highlight specific features that might go unnoticed or be understood differently in a more general reading. Each volume defines two or three specific theories, making them part of the reader's understanding of how diverse meanings may be constructed from a single novel.

Taken collectively, the volumes in the Critical Companions to Popular Contemporary Writers series provide a wide-ranging investigation of the complexities of current best-selling fiction. By treating these novels seriously as both literary works and publishing successes, the series demonstrates the potential of popular literature in contemporary culture.

Kathleen Gregory Klein
Southern Connecticut State University

1

The Life of Gloria Naylor

The signature trait that connects each of Gloria Naylor's five novels is the transcendence of boundaries. Forever challenging the arbitrary limitations that society imposes on the individual, whether racially motivated, gender-driven, or caste-generated, Naylor demands that her characters question their circumstances in order to change them. Believing that attempts to circumscribe human movement and human interaction result in ultimate dehumanization, Naylor argues for vigilance in dismantling any and all imprisoning forces. Likewise, Naylor's life, from the very beginning, is a testament to the act of defiance.

Born January 25, 1950, in New York City, Gloria Naylor escaped, by mere weeks, birth in the segregated South. Her mother, Alberta McAlpin Naylor, had decided months before her first child's arrival that the baby would not be born in the mother's native Robinsonville, Mississippi, or in any other southern place. In a 1986 interview between Naylor and her parents, Naylor's mother reveals her determination not to raise any child in Mississippi for fear of limited opportunities for educational growth and advancement. Therefore, in December 1949, Alberta and husband Roosevelt, following Alberta's parents who had already gone to New York several months before, departed Mississippi for New York in search of better jobs and more fulfilling personal lives.

The Naylors were a part of the second Great Migration, that post–World War II phenomenon whereby scores of black southerners joined with those who had migrated north in a previous generation to escape southern violence and political and economic disenfranchisement. *Brown v. Board of Education*, the transformative court case of the twentieth century that would dismantle legalized racial segregation, would not come to fruition until 1954, while voting rights and other civil rights initiatives would not take effect until the mid-1960s.

For many blacks, moving north offered more immediate remedies to social ills. With Roosevelt as a motorman with the New York City Transit Authority and Alberta as a telephone operator, the Naylors worked tirelessly to ensure their children a life far better than the one they had known. The Naylors' dreams were simple: provide a stable home life for their family, which would ultimately include three daughters. For Roosevelt the agenda was basic and unadorned: "Coming from a place like Mississippi, what you thought about more or less was to go to *a* place, get *a* job, and have *a* weekly paycheck. A steady job and place to live" (Naylor "Reflections"). Although the Naylors enjoyed a few more social freedoms than they did in the South, Roosevelt was thrust immediately back into the Jim Crow system of legal racial segregation when he was drafted into the army in the very early 1950s during the Korean conflict. Ironically, the Truman administration outlawed segregation in the armed forces just as Roosevelt was discharged.

Conceived in one region and one decade, yet born in others, Naylor entered life in transcendence. Commenting that her "conception in the South has played the more important role in shaping [her] life as a writer" (in Colby 636), Naylor confirms the significance of her dual heritage in her outlook on the world about which she writes. Because of her family's immediate southern roots, her own northern perspective, and to some degree her place as the oldest child, Naylor has always viewed life broadly and critically. Her precocious nature as a child is easily attributed to all of these factors.

Naylor's interest in literature was generated at an early age when her mother, an avid reader who was denied access to the public library before she left the South, encouraged young Gloria to read broadly. Her penchant for writing was revealed as early as age seven when she would write poems to express feelings she found difficult to utter. By age twelve she describes herself as a brooder, a gifted child, and a voracious reader, who used writing as a means for venting various feelings and frustrations. As she matured, reading and writing would continue to soothe her creative urges and provide Naylor with a forum for considering her own opinions about the world around her. Sequestering herself in the attic of her parents' house, the preteen Gloria would pull a sheet across part of the space and call it Gloria's Gallery. There she wrote poems and bits of prose to satisfy this predilection for creativity. She even began drafting a novel at sixteen, though no complete work materialized. Naylor describes her early reading as being indiscriminate. When she was thirteen, however, her seventh-grade teacher gave her a copy of Charlotte Brontë's *Jane Eyre*, insisting that every young woman should read this classic before her fourteenth birthday. From this point on, Naylor was eager to read more classic literature. By the time she entered high school, her teachers had begun to sharpen her reading tastes, but although Naylor continued to read enthusiastically all required books for her classes, her increased work with church activities curtailed somewhat her leisure reading (in Wilson "Interview").

As the oldest child, young Gloria always felt the need to see and know more than did her younger sisters. She even acknowledges the necessity of intuiting the moods of others around her, especially her mother and father, in order to understand, and in turn make harmonious, her family life. Naylor recalls the Christmas season 1959, when her parents were still telling the three children about Santa Claus, admitting that "for their sakes" she had pretended to go along with the ruse for a good two years, since age seven. Smug in her knowledge, young Gloria enjoyed a "perverse pleasure" in disregarding the fairy tales her parents still shared in an attempt to protect an innocence the adult Gloria can never remember having. Naylor always remembers seeing beyond, or through, any artifice. In large measure, her maturity was the result of her having always to be the responsible child. As she recalls, the family mantra was always, "Gloria, you're old enough to know better" (in Wilson "Interview"), whenever her parents felt frustrated with the misbehavior of any of the daughters. A young Naylor was always held accountable not only for her own actions, but also for those of her younger sisters, one and five years her junior.

Naylor's ability to see and appreciate life beyond her own limited world was sharpened more in 1962, when she was twelve, after Alberta and her three daughters became Jehovah's Witnesses. In keeping with this faith, the Naylors stopped celebrating Christmas. As a consequence, Gloria found herself different from most of those around her, particularly her peers. In this role as "other," Naylor strengthened her resolve to be true to her convictions, taking pride in her new religious zeal. Later in her teen and early adult years, she was even relieved that she did not have to participate in the frenzied pace of the holiday season. Her Jehovah's Witness status provided her a vantage point from which to view behaviors, actions, and rituals that others would simply call normal. Yet as a Witness, Naylor came to understand that there are different modes of normalcy. For her, not celebrating Christmas was normal, and the accelerated pace of holiday movement was strange. By 1992, at age forty-two, Naylor relished the holiday season because she enjoyed the silence. Though no longer a Witness, her legacy from that experience is to treat the holiday as just another day: "I don't have to go on a frantic search to fill up the spaces of time with anybody doing anything to avoid what is not" (in Naylor "Hers" Dec. 20, 1992).

Naylor views her childhood as a time of learning and preparation. Her parents taught her that no matter what life doles out, one must do his or her personal best to succeed. Naylor recalls that her parents and their extended circle of family and friends had absolutely no sympathy for anyone who lacked self-respect. They acknowledged the possibility of hard times for anyone, but they did not condone voluntary submission to life's difficulties. Parents who neglected children, persons who refused to seek gainful employment, those who shamed themselves and others by using too much foul language in public were treated as "trifling" and not fit for association. In reviewing her parents' lives, both in the South and in New York, Naylor has come to understand the importance of personal sacrifice in exchange for future reward. Though her parents hoped merely to survive with their dignity intact, Naylor knows that the more expansive dreams she has not only imagined, but also achieved, are the result of her parents' humble determination (in Naylor "Reflections"). The one lesson Naylor cherishes from her parents is that each daughter was to decide for herself her particular journey in life and to pursue it with passion and determination. They were to allow no one to dissuade them from their goals or make them feel inferior or unequal to the task at hand. "We were told that we had value; our lives meant something, and we should do something meaningful" (in Wilson "Interview").

Naylor remembers her childhood as a time when she was introduced to the power of language, especially the spoken word. Even as an accomplished writer in the present, Naylor bemoans the ultimate impotence of the written word as compared to the richness of speech (in Naylor "Hers" Feb. 20, 1986). Nevertheless, it is her general appreciation of language that would compel Naylor to become a writer. Surrounded by an extended family, composed of aunts, uncles, cousins, grandparents, and assorted friends, Naylor was bombarded with speech as all of the different voices clamored for attention and vied for authority on the topic of the moment. Naylor and her parents lived in the Bronx and in Queens during her formative years, though they often spent much time in what Naylor calls the "weekend mecca" of her maternal grandparents' Harlem apartment, located on the ground floor of one of the buildings they owned. In this space, Naylor learned that spoken language was more powerful because it could change the meaning of a given word or set of words with a mere shift in voice, inflection, or tone.

Fascinated with this complexity, Naylor found herself trying to understand the richness and its effect on the speakers as well as the listeners. While in the third grade, Naylor was met with a particular challenge in this regard. Upon receiving a test grade higher than the one received by one of her white schoolmates, Naylor suffered the insult of being called "nigger." She had heard this word used frequently and loosely, with humorous or even endearing intent, in the confines of her own community, but she sensed a different meaning coming from her classmate. This was one of her first lessons about audience, intent of speech, tone, and listener response, all tools on which a budding writer would later depend. Going to her mother feeling humiliated by the insult, Naylor was given a brief lesson on the differences of people and the differences in language. Because of her mother's sensitivity and care, Naylor was strengthened by the experience, ultimately concluding that words themselves (especially written ones) are innocent; it is the speaker and/or the listener who empowers them. By the time she was in high school, Naylor began to appreciate the written word and its ongoing struggle, and consistent success, in echoing the richness of spoken language.

A growing need to understand people and life circumstances compelled Naylor to assume an unlikely challenge upon finishing high school. Graduating in 1968 with honors from Andrew Jackson High School in Queens, just two months after the assassination of Martin Luther King, Jr., Naylor, a committed Jehovah's Witness, set out on a seven-year missionary excursion that took her back intermittently to her southern roots, in particular North Carolina and Florida. Given the tension-filled climate of the country at the time, Naylor decided that it was not the right time to attend college. "After the assassination, one of my teachers in high school cried in front of the class and said, 'You know there's a cancer spreading in this country and I want you to go home and think about what that means.' I went home and I did that. And I said, the cancer's not only in this country, that cancer is in the world" (in Goldstein 35). Her work with the Jehovah's Witnesses strengthened the foundation that her parents had established long before. She was taught yet again to value the human spirit and potential, and to care about others whether or not they reciprocated the feelings. The church also taught her that each human being has an important mission in life and that he or she must use native talents to carry out that mission. Naylor still believes that even if one does not follow the tenets of a particular religion, the structure and moral grounding of formal religions are important for establishing and teaching basic values (in Wilson "Interview"). She also credits her work with the Witnesses for helping her to shed her shy personality.

After her zeal for missionary work waned, Naylor returned to New York in 1975 and enrolled in college, initially at Medgar Evers College where she studied nursing for a short time and ultimately at Brooklyn College (while working at various hotels as a telephone operator). In college, Naylor emerged from being the very good student she had been in elementary and high school to being a self-described "excellent and more focused" student, mainly as a result of her age (mid- to late twenties) and life experience (in Wilson "Interview"). During this time two important events occurred. She began writing seriously, and she married. These two developments, each at cross-purposes with the other, converged to alter her life forever. In November 1979, two months before her thirtieth birthday, Naylor was notified that *Essence* magazine would publish her short story, "A Life on Beekman Place," in the spring. Editor Marcia Gillespie encouraged her to continue writing, if she did nothing else in life. Naylor was both pleased and frightened. To be told that she truly had talent, yet to think about a life that would require her to produce, terrified the budding writer. The following month, just one month shy of her birthday, Naylor accepted a proposal of marriage, thinking that she would rather travel down the known road of marriage rather than trek down the uncharted terrain of writing professionally. For her, marriage was conventional and safe, especially with age thirty looming on the horizon. Later, Naylor would admit that she was actually more concerned with *getting* married than with *being* married. As a consequence, the marriage was soon dissolved. During its short term, however, Naylor found herself feeling confined and compromised in not only a male-dominated domestic space, but also a patriarchal world, an obstacle she would tackle again and again.

In 1981 Naylor graduated from Brooklyn College with a B.A. in English. With the advance from her publisher for *The Women of Brewster Place* (1982), Naylor rewarded herself with a trip to Algeciras in southern

Spain. She admits attempting to emulate revered writers who made different areas of Europe their own (Ernest Hemingway, Barcelona; or James Baldwin, Paris, for example). She expected to see Europe the way these writers had, but as a woman, she was harassed for traveling alone. From that time forward, Naylor resented the double standard forced on women in society. Her sense of defiance as a woman in general, as a black woman in particular, crystallized. As a result Naylor came to admire women who, with a little selfish intent, deliberately defy convention, not to the point of self-destruction, but only for self-affirmation (in Naylor and Morrison).

By the time Naylor completed college in 1981 she was already published. As indicated above, *Essence* magazine had published in March 1980 her short story "A Life on Beekman Place," which would later become the "Lucielia Louise Turner" chapter in *The Women of Brewster Place*. Receiving a fellowship, Naylor immediately entered the M.A. program at Yale University in 1981, submitting for her thesis what would become her second novel, *Linden Hills* (published 1985), and earning her degree in 1983. Attending Yale was a matter of opportunity and choice. When asked why she decided on Yale, she always states, very pragmatically, that it was the scholarship. While partially true (Naylor was also offered a fellowship at Cornell), Naylor attended Yale also because of its proximity to New York, allowing her to remain near her close-knit family. Naylor's stint at Yale was almost cut short at the end of her second year when she decided not to return. During her first year Naylor had found difficulty in reconciling her scholarly world with her creative world. Sitting in classes where she was expected to analyze texts incessantly, Naylor discovered that her own creative endeavors were hampered. Only when the graduate faculty agreed that her *Linden Hills* manuscript could serve as her thesis did she agree to return. When asked what she considers her greatest personal accomplishments, without hesitation Naylor proudly announces that she is happy to have completed her master's degree, and she is particularly proud of having completed both *The Women of Brewster Place* and her undergraduate degree within the same month. According to Naylor, she had, for the first time in her life, finished a project successfully and, as a consequence, gained invaluable confidence (in Wilson "Interview"). And at the dawn of the twenty-first century Naylor is pleased with her twenty-year success as a writer.

After publishing *Linden Hills*, Naylor felt that she could truly call herself a writer. Even though she would have to reassure her mother periodically that she would not starve because she would never have a "steady" job, Naylor is confident that she has chosen the right life for herself. Fully aware that she could use her talents in other ways, she believes that she has no choice but to write. According to Naylor, life would be very flat if she could not immerse herself into this very important work. Because she views herself as a transcriber, or a filter, "everything [she's] ever lived or wanted to live as a black woman comes out in [her] work" (in Rowell 188). Admitting that the writing life is a solitary life, Naylor finds that she thrives in that quiet space that writing requires. She enjoys not only the quiet that must surround her, but also the quiet in her mind and spirit. The writing life is so inextricably bound to her real life that she can no longer distinguish between the two. Her characters, whom she admires and respects, people her real world, and in order to interact with them, she must protect this quiet life.

She admits that she is quite fortunate in her ability to create her own environment, to welcome the interruptions she likes and to resist those potential intrusions that might disrupt her life and craft. Naylor rejoices in those sources that inspire and energize her. She likes the fall season, because it reminds her of her childhood anticipation of the new school year, which she always looked to with exhilaration. Music also comforts her, and with an eclectic taste (opera, jazz, rhythm and blues), she is never bored, especially since she has inherited an exhaustive library of albums from her father, who also touted a diverse musical taste. The only element in life that truly unnerves Naylor, and one that she always tries to keep at bay, is human stupidity, which she defines as "the refusal to look beyond one's tiny horizons and to interpret the world only from one's small point of view" (in Wilson "Interview"). At this stage of her life, however, interaction with such people or opinions is practically nonexistent. Of course, Naylor is affected by what she considers a determined bias against the arts in America. Stemming from narrow-mindedness, according to Naylor, this negative treatment has resulted in the repeated slashing of arts budgets, especially that of the NEA (National Endowment for the Arts). Naylor bemoans America's cultural insensitivity, though she hopes that one day this country will uphold the arts in the same way that some other countries do.

At this stage of life (Naylor turned fifty in 2000), Naylor has only two key interests, her writing and her family. Never remarrying and having no children of her own, Naylor is close to her mother and her two sisters, the youngest of whom maintains quarters in Naylor's expansive Brooklyn, New York, brownstone. As the oldest child, she feels responsible for the welfare of her family. Several years ago, when she was drafting *Bai-*

ley's Cafe, Naylor helped to raise a teenage nephew, altering her usual early-morning writing regimen to a late-night routine in order to oblige his needs. And even now she plans to refurbish her home to accommodate her aging and widowed mother (Naylor's father died in 1993), who plans to return to New York from Charlotte, North Carolina (having moved there in 1991 with her husband when both retired), to spend the remainder of her days close to her children (in Wilson "Interview"). The compassion and commitment to humanity that her parents instilled in a young Gloria now define the middle-aged writer, who has vowed never to place her mother in a nursing home, unless doing so becomes medically necessary.

Naylor's passion for the writing life transcends her need for academic stimulation. Although she could always teach, she does not need teaching. In fact, she has not taught since 1990. She admits unabashedly to the need to write, however. And even though she has taught in various MFA programs around the country (e.g., Princeton, the University of Pennsylvania, Boston University, Brandeis University, and Cornell University) and served as a visiting scholar at the University of Kent in Canterbury, England, Naylor is ambivalent about the necessity of such programs for young writers. She thinks that perhaps they need the structure of an academic setting to ensure their discipline to the craft. But if she had to choose between life experience (whether pumping gas or waiting tables) and academia, she would opt for life experience. Naylor does see the writing life as a means of learning respect. When she is teaching, she respects the vision of her students, just as she demands that they respect her vision. Her role is to help them on the journey that they have mapped out for themselves, just as her mentors helped her. For Naylor, mutual respect should also be a staple in life.

As for Naylor's taste in reading, she enjoys mostly women writers. Her favorites include Louise Erdrich, Paule Marshall, Toni Morrison, Alice Walker, Edwidge Danticat, Octavia Butler, and Margaret Atwood. She also likes the later works of John Irving, from *The Cider House Rules* on (she appreciates the fact that with that novel, Irving begins to take a strong moral stand). Naylor admits that her reading is sporadic. She cannot read fiction when she is writing fiction, preferring at those times either poetry or biography. Her current fiction project and its research demands consume much of her time. This sixth book, a historical novel, will be a "prequel" to *Mama Day*, charting the journey of Bascombe Wade from Norway to America and the journey of Sapphira Wade from Senegal to America, and then tracing their journey together once they meet in Savannah, Georgia. The thematic issues will include slavery, identity, and the role of "masking."

Though now considered one of the premier contemporary writers, Naylor, with modesty and humility, still appreciates both the critical and popular attention her novels have garnered. She admits to having just as much respect for the scholar and critic as she does for her fellow creative writer. As a consequence, she never quibbles with critical interpretations, maintaining instead a confidence that the scholar attempts to critique the subject matter as objectively as possible. She also respects the fact that the critical writer, too, is struggling to create, staring at the blank page (or blank computer screen) just as often as does the creative writer. As with the creative writer, Naylor believes that much of what the critical writer produces is the result of subconscious thought, intellectual processes over which he or she has no direct control. Some twenty years have elapsed since Naylor first began writing in earnest, but she still considers her parents' pride her most cherished compliment, expressed humbly and sincerely in her father's "I didn't know you had this in you" upon reading an early copy of *The Women of Brewster Place* (in Wilson "Interview").

Without a doubt, Naylor's place in American letters is secure, as she was granted two awards in 1983: the American Book Award for Best First Novel for *The Women of Brewster Place* and the annual Distinguished Writer Award from the Mid-Atlantic Writers Association. Other honors have included a National Endowment for the Arts Fellowship in 1985, the 1986 Candace Award from the National Coalition of One Hundred Black Women, a Guggenheim Fellowship in 1988, and the 1989 Lillian Smith Award, Southern Regional Council, for *Mama Day* (1988).

Arguably, the element from her life that has been most influential on her novels is her southern heritage. Even though Naylor was born and raised in the North, she and her family took annual car trips to the South in the summers to visit with relatives (her paternal grandparents and scores of aunts, uncles, and cousins remained there). Naylor found these journeys enjoyable and informative; she was often struck with the politeness of southerners, both black and white. While she admits that the South she found probably differed radically from the one her parents had fled, she still credits the white southerners whom she encountered for their humanity and kindness. As a child, she was struck with the slower pace of the South, but as she matured, Naylor realized that almost every other place, regardless of region, is slower than New York City. Naylor has continued to travel south in her adult years. That her parents removed to North Carolina upon their retirement is a testament to the family's long-term attachment to, and respect for, their southern roots.

Understanding that southern life in many ways defines the African-American experience, Naylor feels obligated to capture this essence in all of her works. And though she knows that not every black experience is southern or working class, especially in the second half of the twentieth century, she affirms the southern scape as an inescapable foundation. While *The Women of Brewster Place* is ostensibly set in a northern urban center that tests the fortitude and resilience of the title characters, it is apparent that for several of the women, southern roots and southern experience inform their powers of survival. Major characters Mattie Michael, Etta Mae Johnson, Lucielia Louise Turner, and Ben all hail from Tennessee; and Theresa is from Georgia. Like Naylor's parents, these characters have come north in search of a more fulfilling life; unlike the Naylors, however, many of these characters find their desires, if not thwarted, then indeed deferred.

Linden Hills is set in the same northern city as is *The Women of Brewster Place*, but there is still the slight southern "intrusion" on the narrative space. Linden Hills' existence defines the founding residents' response to southern memories of segregation and subjugation: the upscale black neighborhood was established in utter defiance to racism and white authority. On the other hand, the southern home is presented as the grounding identity for the black psyche, that place which speaks truth and disdains superficiality. When Laurel Dumont, corporate executive, returns to Georgia after an elapsed period of time to visit Roberta Johnson, the grandmother who practically raised her, and behaves like a stranger in the old woman's house, Roberta snidely remarks, "Miss, my cups and glasses are where they been for the last thirty years. If anything's changed, it ain't them" (230). The black southern sensibility figures significantly, then, in the general atmosphere of Linden Hills.

The third novel, *Mama Day* is set primarily in the South. It strives not only to reestablish the primacy of southern place in African-American identity, but also to position African cosmology as a legitimate means of viewing the world. The very title of the novel establishes the centrality of African conjuring ritual. Miranda (Mama) Day, as resident practitioner of the occult, reminds other characters, and the reader, of the importance of fidelity to one's cultural (both regional and ethnic) foundation. Though Cocoa, Mama Day's great-niece, has moved to New York, her new life must never eclipse what is considered her more authentic identity.

Bailey's Cafe is the most unique of Naylor's novels, because it depends most heavily on the reader's imaginative powers. Instead of the setting being fixed, it is virtual, moving from city to city as the narrative dictates. This flexibility accommodates Naylor's signature transcendence. None-theless, no matter what the setting is and how the reader visualizes it, there are still reminders that the southern/northern paradigm is at work. When confronted with the problem of finding a job in a racially preju-diced society, Stanley (a.k.a. Miss Maple) soon determines that he might as well have tried seeking employment below the Mason-Dixon line, because he realizes that the forty-eight contiguous states are "all *south* of the Canadian border." What initially seems to be a slight "directional" cue reminds the reader of its "geographical" implications. Once again, the novel proper sustains a southern intrusion.

Naylor's fifth novel, *The Men of Brewster Place*, also applies this south-ern foundation. In a work that focuses on black manhood, it is important for Naylor to address the origins of black male oppression, and she does so by resurrecting the voice of Ben (a southern black male who died in *The Women of Brewster Place*) to narrate. Ben reminds the reader not only of his own personal oppression in Tennessee by white male authority, but also of the history of black male oppression, when he relates the childhood plight of his grandfather and the man's ensuing bitterness throughout life. This southern history, then, impacts the lives, if only indirectly, of the other men in the novel.

With regard to subject matter, Naylor maintains that since she hails from a working-class family, she will always include that group in her fiction. She is, however, impressed with black writers who choose also to write about the middle class. After all, according to Naylor, the black community is diverse and all facets of black life should be explored. Both *Linden Hills* and *Mama Day* directly address middle-class issues. As a spate of younger black writers emerge on the literary scene, Naylor be-lieves that more compelling stories about black middle-class and upper-class life will be told. This newer generation, Naylor thinks, will be fur-ther and further removed from its southern roots, and with this shift there will be less interest in those working-class struggles that so often are related to the racial conflicts so well known in the South. Neverthe-less, Naylor argues that any literature worth reading will have to reflect the complex human struggle that is such an inherent component of working-class life.

Because her life, in this present moment, is the culminating event of the ancestral lives who came before her, Naylor is a conduit and voice for the experiences of her forebears. All of those lives "[go] into that filter, and I can't tear it apart or snip it apart and ask: how much of this is a black woman, how much of this is a personal history, how much of this is a racial history? There is no way to know that—there isn't" (in Rowell 188). Blurring of the line between her fiction and her life was manifested as early as her first novel when she used in the text actual house numbers of two buildings in Harlem owned by her grandparents. Naylor's role as writer entails more than just her own personal aspirations; it involves a duty to the lives of not only a family, but also a people.

When *The Women of Brewster Place* was translated into a two-part television miniseries in 1989 and a weekly, though short-lived, ABC series in 1990, produced by Oprah Winfrey, Naylor was ushered into American popular culture. As a result of increased attention to her works, Naylor formed One Way Productions in 1990 (dissolved in 2000 so that she can focus solely on her writing) in order to wield a measure of control over future adaptations of her novels. Her stint as visiting playwright with the Hartford Stage Company in 1994 solidified her interest in developing her skills in drama. And as contributing editor of *Callaloo*, the premier academic journal of African-American arts, and as the editor of *Children of the Night: The Best Short Stories by Black Writers, 1967 to the Present* (1996), Naylor has been instrumental in shepherding the careers of budding young writers and in fashioning the new face of African-American literature for the twenty-first century.

Naylor "feel[s] that we have more in common than we have differences, in terms of gender lines, racial lines, and national lines. We have, of course, attempted to exterminate ourselves over those tiny differences, but they are in fact minor" (in Denison "Interview with Gloria Naylor" 21). As a means of mitigating these differences that various groups have intensified over time, Naylor writes in order to "articulate experiences that want articulating—for those readers who reflect the subject matter, black readers, and for those who don't—basically white middle class readers" in the hope that "there will be some glimpse of understanding" (in Goldstein 36). If any writer can bridge the human divide, there is no doubt that Gloria Naylor can.

2

Literary Heritage

The African-American literary tradition is by definition a tradition of response. It is a reaction to the limitations imposed upon it by so-called mainstream, or European-influenced, literature. For the earliest African-American writer, simply crafting an art in written form was a cause of wonder and curiosity because black people were considered the intellectual inferiors of whites. When Thomas Jefferson stated, in his *Notes on the State of Virginia*, "But never yet could I find that a black had uttered a thought above the level of plain narration," he echoed the majority belief in his day that blacks could not produce any literature worthy of acknowledgment or critique. Every sample of African-American literature written since Jefferson's time has striven to defy notions of inferiority. Knowing that Jefferson could denounce the artistry of his talented contemporary Phillis Wheatley in the latter half of the eighteenth century, African-American writers have long understood that their productions must sustain critical inquiry while at the same time offering a unique perspective to their American experiences.

Phillis Wheatley, the premier African-American poet, serves as the prototype for those who emerge after her. Her role in this regard is significant for two reasons. She proved that she could match the skill of the most revered European poets who preceded her, specifically classical and metaphysical poets. Also, she established early on that the African-American writer is at variance with the white writer simply by virtue of existing. That Jefferson could dismiss her poems as trivial effusions is a testament to the black writer's precarious position, one made more difficult, ironically, with the passage of time. As late as 1926 poet Langston Hughes, in his essay "The Negro Artist and the Racial Mountain," bemoaned the double-edged sword of criticism lodged against the black writer from both black and white audiences—the former expected only positive and purified images of black people and the latter accepted only stereotypes: "The Negro artist works against an undertow of sharp criticism and misunderstanding from his own group and unintentional bribes from the whites" (1270). And still in 1937 Richard Wright's "Blueprint for Negro Writing" exposed white condescension toward black writing and even black disdain for any but the "best" of black creative endeavors, which included any writing that protected black middle-class ideas of art deemed "acceptable" to present to the white public as evidence of black civility.

Following on the heels of Phillis Wheatley, the African-American genre to take precedence at the end of the eighteenth century and well into the nineteenth century was the slave narrative, which was also motivated by the need to respond. The slave narrative was an autobiographical account of a former slave's life in slavery, generally told from his or her earliest remembrance to the point of achieving freedom. While it sought to expose the horrors of that peculiar institution, the slave narrative was also motivated by the narrator's desire to engender a belief in black humanity. That is, crafting a slave narrative entailed two objectives that highlighted the narrator's somewhat paradoxical identity. In divulging the abuses of slavery, narrators had to present themselves as objects of abuse (certainly with no intention of condoning objectification), yet they also wanted to present themselves as "subjects" of their own stories, that is, as agents in their own lives who had the moral and natural right to initiate their freedom.

The slave narrative, then, provides the initial example of a dual African-American identity: on the one hand, marginalized, or objectified, by the majority society; and then on the other hand, repositioned, from the minority perspective, in the role of subject. Appreciating the importance of point of view in the slave narrative is vital in understanding this complex African-American identity. Within the narrative, there is not only a difference between the white perspective of African-American identity and the opposing black perspective, but also a difference between two black perspectives. The slave story is, in fact, a journey marking the slave person's transition from object self to subject self. The object self is the "character" in the story while the subject self is the narrative voice relating the story. It is this narrative voice who ultimately takes precedence and who embodies the true African-American identity, if for no other reason than that this voice is authentic (i.e., told by the black voice for the black experience).

The foremost slave narrator whose work best characterizes subject voice identity is Olaudah Equiano. In his *The Interesting Narrative of the Life of Olaudah Equiano, or Gustavus Vassa, the African. Written by Himself* (1789), Equiano provides a rare glimpse into a former slave's African existence. The first chapter of his story avails the reader of information about the social, political, economic, familial, cultural, and intellectual life of his sophisticated tribal community. By presenting such details, Equiano immediately dismantles stereotypes about savage African life. And when he discloses details concerning his initial encounter with whites, Equiano describes a sudden fear for what he considers a barbaric unknown. In short, Equiano engages in his own brand of defiance, whereby he inverts the accepted principles (definitions) of good/bad, white/black, civilized/savage, subject/object, and standard/alien, respectively. Instead of adopting the European perspective that would categorize everything associated with blackness as savage, or bad, etc., Equiano, with this "inversion," positions himself and his culture as the standard, or normal, entity, from which perspective all else is other, or alien.

When one considers the intellectual foundation of African-American literature, one is struck with its almost inherent association with Modernism. In fact, African-American literature was modern before Modernism. After World War I, Modernism emerged not only as an artistic phenomenon, but also as a general cultural phenomenon that purported to question, to challenge, the norm. In art (written, visual, and otherwise) Modernism initiated stylistic innovations, which included disrupting form, blurring the boundaries among genres, and in the case of the written word, experimenting with syntax, unity, and coherence. In general cultural matters, Modernism interrogated notions of normalcy and tradition. With war casualties approaching global proportions, the postwar world found itself grasping for any semblance of stability. If traditional mores failed, then new modes of being had to be explored. Modernism was contradictory; on the one hand it espoused democratic ideals, but on the other it still tacitly condoned elitism (evident in its condescending embrace of "primitive" art and people). Also, Modernism addressed the plight of the disintegrated human personality, dehumanized by an increasingly insensitive, mechanized environment. In short, Modernism attempted to derive some new sense of order out of a rapidly changing society; hence Modernism is best defined by flux and mystery.

In linking African-American existence to Modernism, Cornel West, Harvard scholar and professor of African-American studies, has observed that African Americans are the most *modern* of all people (*modern* defined as "newness, novelty, and innovation"), because they have had to "revamp, revision, and recast themselves" in response to the obstacles that attempt to impede their economic, social, and even spiritual journey. In this regard, according to West, confinement is the quintessential African-American dilemma, made even more problematic by the fact that "movement" is the most American (European), hence the most traditional, of concepts. If to be normal is to be mobile, then to be confined is to be made abnormal, or to be marginalized. And if one's blackness is normalized as being in a confined position, then one's inherent self, blackness, is made abnormal.

African-American artists (writers), then, from Wheatley in the eighteenth century to artists in the present, have recast themselves by confronting and ultimately surmounting attempts to dehumanize and distort their "inverted" (translated "centered," or normalized) personalities. They have questioned traditional views of their existence and must continue to do so, refashioning themselves, at least in their own minds, as normalized beings. Even before Harlem Renaissance writers in the 1920s gave birth to the identity of the New Negro, the concept had already become a part of the communal African-American identity. The Harlem Renaissance is defined as the first self-conscious artistic movement for African Americans. Resulting in part from the scores of African Americans who migrated north after World War I, and particularly to Harlem, the Renaissance witnessed untold levels and varieties of artistic creation. One defining moment of the movement was the 1925 publication of the anthology *The New Negro*, edited by Alain Locke, who in the introductory essay of the same name clearly defined what he thought should be the twentieth-century African-American personality: independent, self-motivated, culturally grounded, and unapologetic for one's presence or interests. Wheatley, Equiano, Frederick Douglass (leading black intellectual of the nineteenth century), and others had already begun to carve out such an identity long before it was given a specific definition.

It is this literary history that Naylor, like all black writers, must confront and overcome in her artistry. To present the African-American experience in the contemporary moment, Naylor must respond, or react, to preconceived notions of what that experience entails. Just as the black writer's ability was questioned in former times, the authenticity of perspective, particularly when a writer like Naylor challenges stereotypical images, might be questioned in the present moment.

While Modernism may indeed provide a lens through which to consider African-American literature, Postmodernism more accurately frames the impulses that motivate Naylor's novels. Whereas Modernism strove to address emergent social and aesthetic chaos, to challenge old norms, and then to establish (or at least suggest) new ways of seeing and understanding, Postmodernism unabashedly admits its inability (in fact, its unwillingness) to create new unity. Rather, Postmodernism would submit that true artistry should reflect the ongoing, never-to-be-fully-resolved, philosophical, social, intellectual battles that consume all human interaction. While Modernism would blur boundaries in order to establish new boundaries, Postmodernism would question the boundaries completely: caste (or class), gender, racial, political, aesthetic, and so on. Modernism bemoans the psychological fragmentation that accompanies stress-ridden human existence, though Postmodernism, to some degree, celebrates such fragmentation as a phenomenon that potentially democratizes human experience. Social harmony is defined as the acceptance of warring perspectives. From a literary perspective, a novel might end by posing questions instead of offering answers; or a given literary work might not easily be categorized because it employs characteristics of poetry or the essay or drama in an attempt to prod the reader to reconsider the very notion of definitions.

One of the more obvious ways in which Naylor employs the Postmodern is her appropriation of classical texts. As noted above, the Postmodernist challenges aesthetic boundaries, most often described as the difference between so-called high art and low (or popular, or primitive) art. Since, for the Postmodern writer, politics governs all human experience and all human experience is political, then all human expressions (art) of those experiences are valid. High art has no more aesthetic value than does low art. In fact, these very terms become useless. Therefore, those who might want to maintain a distinction between Naylor's African-American art and a Shakespearean play, for example, would be dismissed by the Postmodern perspective as rigid, misguided, and ultimately anti-intellectual.

Naylor capitalizes on this perspective when she structures three of her five novels with three major European works in mind. *Linden Hills* (1985) is reminiscent of Dante's "Inferno" section of his *The Divine Comedy*.

Mama Day (1988) is modeled after Shakespeare's *The Tempest*, while *Bailey's Cafe* (1992) indirectly reenacts Chaucer's *The Canterbury Tales*. By appropriating these traditional texts, Naylor bridges the gap between the European tradition and African-American art. The characters in Naylor's novels confront the same complexities, confusions, and contradictions that the "high art" characters experience, and though Naylor's characters' experiences are defined by their own unique circumstances, one still learns that the intensity of their feelings or their pain or frustration is as poignant as that of any Shakespearean tragic figure. This is not to argue, of course, that these African-American characters require a comparison to European characters in order to achieve legitimacy, but to suggest that this Postmodern application encourages the reader to consider the similarities in all human experience.

While modeling select novels after great European epics, Naylor also borrows from the European novel. For instance, *Linden Hills*, in addition to its Dantean influence, is shaped by three other genres. The most obvious influence is the Gothic novel, defined as a work in which magic and mystery are the prime elements. The setting, characterized by a brooding and unknown terror, is usually a sprawling mansion wherein bizarre and supernatural occurrences abound. In addition to the Gothic novel, Naylor applies traits from the picaresque novel. This genre records the journey of a rascal (the protagonist, known also as a *picaro*) from a low social class who works at menial tasks, though in reality he makes his living more through wit than effort. The novel, while apparently structureless, is episodic (each scene is held loosely together by a connecting thread, generally the protagonist). On his various adventures the picaro encounters persons of varying degree, a narrative construction that allows the author to satirize the social classes. Although her "revision" of the Gothic and picaresque novels is most obvious, Naylor also defers, if only subtly, to the epistolary novel (a novel written as a series of letters) as well as to the ledger and the photograph.

As one proceeds chronologically through Naylor's canon, or body of works, it becomes quite apparent that her novels become more structurally complex and less reliant on traditional forms. In her inaugural novel *The Women of Brewster Place* (1982) Naylor creates a surreal setting by blurring the distinction between illusion and reality, a signature trait in all subsequent texts. In the final chapter, entitled "The Block Party," the women initiate a plan to coerce their absentee landlord to authorize improvements in the otherwise neglected Brewster tenement. The chaos that has defined their past lives seems to be supplanted with a new sense of balance and direction. Only when one nears the end does the reader realize that the chapter was, in fact, a dream sequence. And though the novel ends on a hopeful note that the women will act on the possibilities presented in the dream, the epilogue, entitled "Dusk," suggests different: "Hallways were blind holes, and plaster crumbled into snaggled gaps. Vermin bred in uncollected garbage and spread through the walls" (191). The Brewster residents' lives are left in shambles because, like most human lives, theirs are subject to the political machinations of bloated power, a fact in this novel highlighted in the first sentence of the prologue, entitled "Dawn": "Brewster Place was the bastard child of several clandestine meetings between the alderman of the sixth district and the managing director of Unico Realty Company" (1). Illusion (dreams) in this text, then, is a source of hope, yet the reality of the circumstances is that despair will prevail.

The challenge to reality is also evident in Naylor's sophomore novel *Linden Hills* (1985). The Linden Hills community serves as the residence of upwardly mobile blacks whose very reason for existence seems to be further material advancement. Luther Nedeed, owner of all deeded tracts in the neighborhood, takes pride in having established a black community that rivals many prestigious white communities. His life mission has been, in fact, to refashion (in a Modernist sense, to re-create) the outside perception of black people. This pursuit of the American dream for the black community becomes a nightmare, however, when the majority of the Linden Hills residents seek material acquisition at the expense of emotional stability. Because practically no one in Linden Hills lives authentically (that is, governed by his or her own natural desires), everyone risks losing sanity. This nightmare is inevitable when one considers the dehumanization required by material acquisition. How do individuals measure their own success in this struggle to acquire? It is measured by creating a society whereby individuals compare themselves to those who have less. Consequently, one's own sense of comfort is predicated on another's discomfort. When Luther and his family perish in the climactic inferno scene near the end of the novel, it is the result of his selfish need to control others.

No doubt Naylor's third novel, *Mama Day* (1988), further develops Naylor's emphasis on the surreal. Set on the mystical Willow Springs island, the novel offers the possibility that knowledge might be gained not just by using logic and reason. Intuition, faith, and even the occult are presented as possible repositories of information that, when tapped, may offer solutions in an otherwise irreconcilable situation. *Mama Day* maintains that the more enlightened characters do not limit themselves to only one (in this case, logical) source of knowledge. Though George ultimately decides to participate in the conjuring practices in an effort to save his wife Cocoa, his efforts come too late to save their marriage. While Cocoa does, in fact, recover, George perishes in the attempt. In *Mama Day* clearly the spiritual world, as defined by the particular culture of Willow Springs, is as real and influential as the temporal world. Neither exists successfully without the other. When the tempest all but destroys the island, it is through a connection with the spiritual world that Cocoa finds solace and an eternal connectedness to George.

While *Mama Day* confronts the tension between the spiritual and the temporal, *Bailey's Cafe* is consumed with psychological fragmentation. The patrons who enter the cafe have recently suffered stifling traumas that have rendered distorted personalities. Not one of them finds easy answers to these dilemmas. Functioning (or attempting to function) primarily in a haze of confusion, frustration, and malaise, they are left to their own devices as they try, not necessarily to reverse their circumstances, but merely, to survive. Set in 1948, a year that marks an important moment in American race relations with the recent integration of major league baseball by Jackie Robinson in 1947, *Bailey's Cafe* anticipates the future of the African-American American dream (made nightmarish in *Linden Hills*).

Nonetheless, six years would pass before the groundbreaking *Brown v. Board of Education* decision, and still another twenty years would pass before significant strides toward civil equality would be realized. *Bailey's Cafe*, then, is appropriately set in this mysterious period when African Americans were quite unsure about the future, given the contradictory messages they received regarding America's promise to honor her creed for all citizens. This uncertain future is highlighted when Ph.D.-holding, expert market analyst, yet unemployed Stanley (a.k.a. Miss Maple), in utter frustration, writes home to his father after being patronized by a "liberal" prospective employer: "Change is hope; you've always told me that. I'm a young man; I will see a lot of change. And *that* is what worries me, Papa, because today I had lunch with the future" (212). The paradox that Stanley feels is quite poignant. On the one hand, he is hopeful about the future; on the other hand, if so-called progress is left in the hands of misguided "liberals" who think they have the best interest of the minority in mind, then the future becomes as bleak as the past. Clearly, Stanley is miffed because even though he has acquired the academic *accoutrements* required to position one for further advancement, he is still rendered inferior in the minds of those who have the power to make such decisions.

Her final offering, *The Men of Brewster Place* (1998), marks Naylor's attempt as a woman to plumb the depths of the African-American male psyche. For Naylor to suspend her female perspective and to assume the male perspective as center is to challenge reality. Just as she explores the tensions between the real and the illusory, or between the temporal and the spiritual, in other novels, Naylor challenges the arbitrary distinctions between life and death in this work. Though Ben dies at the end of *The Women of Brewster Place*, Naylor, as revealed in an author's note, "resurrect[s] his spirit and voice to narrate portions of this novel." Here, and in the other novels that bridge warring realities, Naylor validates the longtime African belief in ancestral presence. That Ben is physically dead (or absent) has no bearing on his influence on the lives he touched while temporally present. The connectedness across the distances of time and space once again invokes a surreal quality.

It is obvious that *The Men of Brewster Place* serves as a companion text to Naylor's first novel. Also important to note, however, is the fact that each work in Naylor's canon is linked to another, if only tangentially. Kiswana Browne, a resident in Brewster Place, is actually a native of *Linden Hills*, yet she has decided to live in Brewster by choice, in large measure to defy her parents and their middle-class values, a point of view that one does not fully understand until one has read *Linden Hills*. Willa Nedeed, who perishes in the fire at the end of *Linden Hills*, in some measure at the hands of her maniacal husband Luther, is the cousin of Ophelia (Cocoa) Day from *Mama Day*. Only after reading *Linden Hills* does one fully appreciate Cocoa's determination not to be controlled by a man. Also, Cocoa's husband George, supposedly conceived immaculately, is the wonder child born at the end of *Bailey's Cafe*. Again, only after reading *Bailey's Cafe* does one completely understand George's confusion about his past and his parentage and thus his unwavering need to control, with logic and reason, all aspects of his life. With her entire body of works, then, Naylor creates a fictional universe whereby noted boundaries, rules, and limitations are challenged and defied in the interest of discovering other possibilities. In addition, Naylor verifies the importance of accepting a changing world and maintaining a willingness to receive new knowledge in the interest of growth and development. When one reads a single novel by Naylor, she or he learns, yet when one then links that novel with another (especially when more information is given about a particular character from the first novel), she or he expands that body of knowledge for greater understanding.

Naylor has long had an interest in what she calls "creative drama," and she has incorporated this interest into her own novels. Her appetite for creative drama was whetted by European literature. Even today, she expresses a fondness for Victorian novels, especially *Wuthering Heights* and *Jane Eyre*, in part for their "long, messy stories with loads of drama . . . and different sorts of natural holocausts going on" (in Rowell 180). These seminal texts made a "profound impression" on Naylor, whether it was the distinct moral viewpoint of Thackeray or Dickens or simply the heightened drama: "I, too, am a moral writer whether I want to think about it or not; I do have a point of view. And I write dramatic novels. It's important for me that there be drama. It's not always external drama, but internal drama that is going on" (in Rowell 180).

While European writers introduced Naylor to literature, it was African-American women writers who confirmed for Naylor the relevance of literature to her daily life and ignited her desire to be a writer. Crediting Toni Morrison's *The Bluest Eye* for giving her the courage even to consider a career in writing, it is no surprise that Naylor has often been compared to the Nobel Prize winner. According to Naylor, "The presence of [*The Bluest Eye*] served two vital purposes at that moment in my life. It said to a young poet, struggling to break into prose, that the barriers were flexible; at the core of it all is language, and if you're skilled enough with that, you can create your own genre. And it said to a young black woman, struggling to find a mirror of her worth in this society, not only is your story worth telling, but it can be told in words so painstakingly eloquent that it becomes a song" (in Naylor and Morrison 568). Morrison demurs at the suggestion that she influenced Naylor so directly, stating, "She [Naylor] says my work was critical to her decision to write prose. She believes that, but I know my work may have figured in *when* she would write a novel but not *whether*" (in Naylor and Morrison 592). It is clear, however, that Morrison had a profound impact on Naylor in encouraging her to resist restriction, both externally and internally inflicted.

Morrison's role in bringing Naylor to the fold of the black women's literary tradition (and ultimately the American tradition) is important in understanding not only the tradition itself, but also for an appreciation of the "flexibility" of that tradition, as demonstrated by the ensuing contributions to the tradition. Because Morrison almost single-handedly defines the black women's tradition in the contemporary moment, Naylor, as Morrison aspirant, also centers that tradition. At the same time, however, Morrison is ironically only loosely connected to that formal tradition. When her early novels are compared to the works of Zora Neale Hurston, Morrison has quite often expressed amazement, admitting never having read Hurston prior to writing her first two novels (in Naylor and Morrison 590). Clearly, then, in Morrison's work there is no direct link to a tradition that, if not established by Hurston, was certainly molded by her. Although Morrison argues that she had never read Hurston, scholars can locate various similarities. Because of the association, the credibility of a black women's literary tradition is actually sustained. That Hurston and Morrison would share certain outlooks and depictions, yet maintain no direct literary connection, speaks to the spiritual sisterhood of black women in their contextual struggles and triumphs. It also allows subsequent writers the latitude to shape their contributions without being restricted to (or by) a fixed definition of black women's literature. While it is true that Naylor, like many of her literary sisters, wrote her first novel "to celebrate the female spirit and the ability to *transcend* and also to give a microcosm of Black women in America—Black women who are faced by a wall of racism and sexism" (in Cleage 57), she does so by offering fresh perspectives on many aspects of African-American life.

Whatever the means, it is clear that Naylor's first novel in 1982 thrust her into the literary limelight in a moment of time when black women writers were reshaping the novel form. By 1982, Morrison had published four novels, and in that same year Alice Walker's *The Color Purple* was also published. That Naylor had only recently discovered black literature herself yet was hailed as a fresh new voice in the genre attests to the rapidly changing climate for black literature and to Naylor's unparalleled skill. Her tenure as the new darling of the literary scene was accompanied, however, by some criticism. Both Naylor and Walker came under fire for their allegedly insensitive portraits of black men. And though Naylor did not respond at length to the accusations at the time, she did reveal later that she was concerned about the negative appraisals. In fact, she even restructured the chapter that was the impetus for *The Women of Brewster Place*, "Lucielia Louise Turner," in anticipation of such critical responses. She opens the chapter by focusing on Eugene, the seemingly wayward and emotionally abusive husband whose actions ultimately result in the death of his daughter. Naylor, as she reveals in her conversation with Toni Morrison, hoped to shed light on Eugene's psychological pain and guilty pangs in order to balance the depiction of black men. This concern reveals Naylor's feelings of responsibility to her larger black audience, even though she admits that in writing a book that addresses black women's issues, she should not have to sugarcoat what can often be strained relationships between black women and black men. To present the women's struggles should in no way, according to Naylor, be construed as an assault on black men. This argument coincides seamlessly with Naylor's focus on transcendence. Just as Naylor resists all attempts at fixity, she rejects the "either-or" premise that to highlight the black woman's pain automatically denigrates the black man.

In addition to Morrison early influences on Naylor include Zora Neale Hurston and Ntozake Shange, all of whom she discovered while in college: "Being a writer then was not an unrealizable dream; it was a very plausible goal, because these women were there. They had done it, and I could perhaps add my voice to that whole stream of consciousness" (in Rowell 179). Although Naylor passionately defends the importance of the European writers in laying a foundation for her education and her craft, she insists that her "home" (her African-American community of women writers) provided her with the courage to pursue the craft: "When I read Edgar Allan Poe, something clicked. When I read Charles Dickens, something clicked. And what was clicking . . . was just, I think, my own birthing. I was waiting to be able to deliver. That would not have been possible if I had not gone on to discover . . . writers who reflected me and my life" (in Rowell 180). The necessity of maintaining ties with her "community" was manifested early in Naylor's writing career when she decided, quite fortuitously, to attend Yale instead of Cornell in order to remain fairly close to home. While at Yale, Naylor, would sometimes take the train into New York to get away from the campus setting.

It is not surprising that Naylor would depend on other black women writers to encourage her own creative pursuits, especially when one considers that Naylor was initially frightened of novel writing. She insists that her real attempt at novel writing did not occur until she set out to produce her third book, *Mama Day*. Referring to her first two novels as compilations of interconnected stories, Naylor maintains that *Mama Day* marked her first effort at generating a sustained story line. With the first two "novels," she simply sought to write one story, then another, then another, comforted that she could produce something by taking ministeps. And although she had the first four novels in mind (she refers to them as her "quartet") when she drafted the first, she did not consciously approach the novel structure until *Mama Day*. While Naylor initially rejected formally adopting the novel as her creative venue, she allows that she always enjoyed reading in the genre, because it affords her and other readers the opportunity to enter a whole universe that they are "attempting to make sense out of."

Because writers are responsible for creating this universe, they are, according to Naylor, given some imaginative latitude while, ironically, also being burdened with external demands. Because fiction is limited by "the convention that it be probable" (in Rowell 181), the fiction writer is expected to honor, to some degree, the reader's realistic sensibilities, even though, insists Naylor, life often renders occurrences more bizarre than those expressed in fiction. And depicting those events often forces the writer to defy reader/audience expectations in honor of the aesthetic product. Honoring the art may also entail challenging the reader's notions of what determines an authentic narrative. For modern and contemporary writers like Naylor who manipulate creative conventions, a narrative may be any end result that the writer produces, whether or not it resembles what the reader has previously encountered. For Naylor, narrative is "anything which drives the story forward, whether it's language or characters' internal dialogue. Lack of [an overt] plot does not necessarily mean a piece of work is missing a narrative. Nor does lack of storyline. But to me plot and storyline are really the same thing" (in Rowell 182). In short, every fictive work has a story line, some mechanism whereby the reader can chart development, and this movement, this development, even if it rests in a character's thoughts, is the plot.

For Naylor, character is the dominant fictional element, and any substantive work must be character-driven. "Characters are running around being themselves. It is the writer's obligation to figure out what these actions mean" (in Rowell 182). In Naylor's creative world the primacy of character is important both before and during the actual writing process. In several interviews Naylor has recounted the impetus for *Bailey's Cafe*. While listening to Duke Ellington's "Mood Indigo," Naylor began to envision two people dancing in a haze on a pier, and this vision kept haunting her dreams. The two people would become characters Sadie and Iceman. Naylor admits that with these two and with all of her other characters, she must interact spiritually with them, going as far as actually drafting letters expressly to certain characters, asking for their guidance as she fleshes out their lives. The characters become quite real to Naylor, so real, in fact, that they sometimes have agendas of their own. Commenting often on Willa Nedeed from *Linden Hills*, Naylor admits that she thought she had determined what Willa's ultimate response would be to her sadistic husband once she escaped her confinement in the basement of the Nedeed home. Though Naylor had planned for Willa to stand up to Luther and then leave the house, Willa "decided" to go upstairs and clean her house in an attempt to restore domestic harmony. Naylor admits to being shocked, disappointed, and frustrated by the actions of a woman who suffered deliberate emotional and physical abuse at the hands of husband Luther and who seemed to develop a more defiant persona in the ensuing months of her imprisonment. But ultimately honoring her commitment to a character-driven text, Naylor had to allow Willa her own voice and her own agenda.

Naylor sees her role as black woman writer as an important canon-shaping endeavor. In her estimation, without black women writers there would be no true American literature. If this literature consisted only of white male writers, then it would not be representative of actual American demographics. Black women writers, and all other previously silenced "marginal" voices, enrich the American identity whether or not the majority acknowledges the contribution. And while Naylor appreciates the legitimate claim that other minorities make about their contributions to American culture and identity, she is responsible only for the black female voice and whatever other black utterances may "filter" through that voice (in Rowell 190).

Without question Naylor has fixed her place within the American canon and the American classroom. Confident in her position, Naylor no longer worries about her legitimacy alongside other writers. Her focus is solely on the project at hand, and when she is immersed in either research or actual writing, she has little time or energy to obsess over her longevity. Admitting that after *The Women of Brewster Place* she feared she might be a one-book wonder, Naylor felt validated and vindicated upon completion of *Mama Day* (for having consciously tackled the novel format) and *Bailey's Cafe* (for honoring her initial commitment to herself to complete her quartet): "I felt that by writing those four books, I would go through an apprenticeship to my craft. Then I would feel, within myself, that I was a writer. When I finished the last of that quartet, it was an exciting, exciting moment for me, to realize that I had set that goal and achieved it. You know, a whole lot can happen in ten years of an adult life, and I had written through all of that" (in Denison "Interview with Gloria Naylor" 21). In revealing her desire that her writing outlive her and reveling in the increased critical inquiry about her work,

Naylor directs her attention to producing other works in the future that will both challenge and interest her readers.

It is important to contextualize Naylor's canon in regard to the social climate that framed her early writing career. As stated earlier *The Women of Brewster Place* was published in the same year that Alice Walker's *The Color Purple* was published. Both texts were largely criticized by black men as having vilified the black male image. While Walker's novel presented the struggle of Celie who endured untold emotional and physical abuse at the hands of her stepfather and later her husband Mister (a.k.a. Albert), Naylor's first novel, of course, details the struggles of several black women whose abject lives result in part from dysfunctional relationships with men. Naylor and Walker do not deliberately attack black men, although they do in fact assail the patriarchal institutions that belittle women, black women in particular. It was their desire to interrogate the interior lives of everyday black women and present a realistic portrait of these women while dismantling gender/racial stereotypes. Dismissing the caricatures of the mammy, the spitfire, the religious zealot, and the trollop, these writers chose instead to consider substantive lives rather than surface images.

Understanding that the 1970s and 1980s feminist movement was in large measure less useful to black women, Walker, Naylor, and other contemporary black women writers (Toni Morrison included) realized that black women needed to establish their own criteria for liberation. To distinguish between the white women's movement and an emergent black women's crusade, Walker even coined the term "womanist" to substitute for "feminist." If the feminist movement concerned itself with white women's right to employment outside the home, birth control, child care, and pay commensurate to their skills and equal to that of men, the womanist movement teased out those racial/gender issues that for time immemorial plagued the black woman.

In *In Search of Our Mothers' Gardens* Walker defines "womanist" as "[u]sually referring to outrageous, audacious, courageous, or *willful* behavior. Wanting to know more and in greater depth than is considered 'good' for one. . . . Responsible. In charge. *Serious*" (xi). The womanist then, by definition, tackles issues that others would rather ignore or dismiss. That the womanist would even separate herself from feminism is an audacious act, but the womanist would submit that the black woman and the white woman have little in common in regard to the struggle for equal rights. While white women fought for the right to work, black women already worked, and indeed had to work, outside the home. While white women demand decent child care, it is the black woman who has often served as care provider in white homes. While white women battle for equal pay (generally to supplement the household income), the black woman simply wants a decent wage, quite often as the single provider; or she might even want a decent wage for her own husband before she joins in a campaign for equal pay for women, particularly if the women who will mainly benefit are white. In short, the womanist perspective clearly appreciates a difference in black women's and white women's lives.

Naylor's and Walker's focus, then, on the interior lives of black women is a key element of womanist belief. They choose to address that part of black women's lives that has little to do with the outside white world. To address the struggles that are a part of black women's domestic lives is in no way an attempt to categorically demean black men. Rather it is an attempt to analyze the plight of the black woman. To understand this present-day plight, one must consider the historical dimensions of black women's American persecution and the ensuant legacy. In the days of slavery black women were defined by their sexual availability to their white owners, a circumstance that rendered them victimized from all sides. White men regarded them as sexual commodities; black men often despised them for "succumbing" to white male rape; and white women blamed the black woman for "seducing" white men. Consequently, the black woman found herself without solace from external sources, and her only recourse was to find even a modicum of peace in her interior life.

In *The Women of Brewster Place* and in *The Color Purple*, Naylor and Walker, respectively, consider this perpetual victimized status. Naylor, in particular, reexamines this interaction between black men and black women. *Mama Day*, for instance, focuses primarily on a redemptive marital relationship. And the main narrator in *Bailey's Cafe* is presented as a sensitive and compassionate man who painfully retells the horrors that have beset the women in the novel. And certainly *The Men of Brewster Place* serves as Naylor's direct attempt to remedy black men's and women's relationships by considering the men's point of view. In this way Naylor offers hope for black women and men, yet she, along with other women writers, insists that such amelioration will not be realized by ignoring the problems.

On this subject Naylor and her contemporaries owe deference to predecessor Zora Neale Hurston, foremost woman writer of the Harlem

Renaissance and the period following. Hurston, too, addressed the domestic struggles of black women, most notably in her novel *Their Eyes Were Watching God* and in her often anthologized short story "Sweat." The novel's protagonist Janie Crawford suffers the emotional and physical abuse of her second husband Joe Starks. And Delia Sykes in "Sweat" endures a similar life. Both women, however, ultimately find themselves relieved of their antagonistic husbands, and in some ways, they are made stronger as a result of their journeys. The narrative similarities between Hurston and her literary progeny do not end here, however. Naylor, like Hurston, presents the lives of her black characters almost at the total exclusion of the outside white community. Hurston was even criticized, particularly by Richard Wright, for not addressing more comprehensively the impact of race and racism on the lives of black people. Hurston, however, answered this charge by suggesting that to harp continually on racism inadvertently intensifies the power that whites have over blacks. Instead, Hurston wanted to focus on those moments in black life when blacks do not think about whites or their efforts at supremacy. In this way, Hurston believed that she, to some degree, liberated her characters. Likewise, Naylor, in the contemporary moment, impels her black characters to interact without direct white interception.

White absence forces black male characters to answer for their abuse without the luxury of scapegoating racism. As is true when black women reject the white feminist agenda, relieving black men of their scapegoat compels black men and women to grapple with their shared issues/concerns. Black women spurn feminist tenets mainly because they see white women as lashing out at men in general (including black men), when black women understand that their gripe is with *white* patriarchy. For black women, gender *and* race are a matter of concern, and they cannot ignore race. And firmly believing that white women do not welcome attempts by black women to expand the feminist agenda to include race, and fully knowing that ultimately white women will abandon black women in reconciliation with their husbands when their true allegiance is questioned/challenged, black women know where their allegiances must lie. If black women, then, abandon "whiteness" (white feminism) in the interest of black female empowerment (which ultimately leads to black racial empowerment), they will not condone black male use of "whiteness" as an excuse for domestic abuse. This is quite obvious in the case of Brewster Place residents Mattie Michael and Ciel Turner. Though Mattie attempts to protect her son Basil from all external attacks and though Ciel defends her husband Eugene from the criticism of others, each woman, in private conversations with each man, holds him accountable for his actions, regardless of his stressful interaction with the outside white world. These black women must hold these individual men accountable, because if they did not, they would, in turn, excuse the white men who maintain a racist social order. If the black woman allows the black man to argue, "I just can't stop myself from abusing you because I'm so victimized by 'the white man,' " she would allow the white male to be excused for his dehumanizing actions. The womanist agenda not only disallows such excuses, but also exposes such excuses for the weaknesses they are, black or white. Neither the black woman nor the black man can sidestep communication with each other by relying on whiteness as a crutch, no matter which one attempts to do so.

One must note, however, that just as Naylor challenges her black characters to overcome racist obstacles, she still acknowledges the long-term power of these obstacles. Nowhere is this observation more evident than in *The Men of Brewster Place*. Addressing the issue of black manhood, Naylor understands the historical persecution of black manhood as a means of destroying the entire black community. This novel responds to the social reality of the past, as it also expands the canon of African-American literature devoted to this issue. From slavery to the present day, the state of black manhood has been used to gauge black success. On the heels of the Civil War, black men were led to believe that they just might be allowed to participate fully as American citizens and thus restore humanity to the black community.

Following the end of the Civil War, Congress passed three significant amendments, informally called the "Civil War Amendments." The Thirteenth Amendment (1865) officially abolished slavery; the Fourteenth Amendment (1868) guaranteed due process under the law and defined U. S. citizenship; and the Fifteenth Amendment (1870) guaranteed citizens the protection of rights against federal or state infringement regardless of race or previous servitude, enfranchising black males throughout the Union. Already in 1867 Congress had passed the Reconstruction Act, which prohibited Southern states from barring black males from voting.

By the beginning of the 1870s, African-American men held, for the first time, positions in all levels of government, including the House of Representatives, the Senate, and even one brief gubernatorial seat in Louisiana. Unfortunately, such success would be short-lived. Southern states, incensed that a race so recently enslaved would enjoy even a modicum of political clout, sought ways to repeal these newly achieved rights. Terrorist groups, like the Ku Klux Klan and local white rifle clubs, emerged with the sole intention of intimidating blacks and curtailing their freedoms. In addition, state and local political machines crafted "legal" methods of circumventing federal law. Once Reconstruction officially ended in 1877, and federal troops were removed from the South, freedmen found themselves without immediate allies like the Freedmen's Bureau, which had been charged with easing the transition from slavery to freedom by educating the former slave and equipping him with marketable skills.

Now at the mercy of angry Southern whites, blacks (men in particular) were left with little recourse. Many had to resort to sharecropping, which was a form of legalized economic slavery. In this system, a black man (along with his family) would rent a parcel of land from a wealthy landlord who would also provide supplies, at an exorbitant price, to the tenant, with the agreement that when the tenant harvested his crop, he would repay the landlord. But because the landlord maintained exclusive rights to all accounting documentation, the tenant always found himself in arrears. Year after year, as the tenant tried desperately to repay the landlord, he only accumulated more debt. This system worked well for landowners because they maintained a constant supply of cheap labor.

Still another invidious method for dehumanizing blacks and retarding their upward mobility was the convict-lease system. In the 1880s and 1890s this became the most notorious method of reenslaving black men. Under this system black men could be arrested for such petty "offenses" as loitering (which often entailed only two or three black men gathering in a public place to talk) or neglecting to allow a white person the right-of-way on a sidewalk. Or if a black man tried to defend himself and protect his federal rights, he was charged with threatening a white person, an egregious offense in the South. After being convicted of the alleged crime, black men were placed on chain gangs or on strenuous work details, repairing roads, railroads, or maybe even refurbishing the sheriff's house.

Then by the turn of the century, and for quite a time thereafter, black men—and more than a few women—were lynched for any number of reasons, or simply because a white mob felt justified in doing so. All of these postbellum efforts were designed to denigrate the black man and discourage him from demanding those rights promised in the Civil War Amendments. By the time of the 1950s Civil Rights Movement blacks were subjected, in addition to continued physical violations, to poll taxes and literacy tests, efforts designed to discourage them from registering to vote.

Naylor, of course, confronts this social reality in *The Men of Brewster Place*, and in doing so she contributes to a genre that has also focused on black manhood, always reminding the reader that whatever affects black manhood affects the larger black community. The two classical American (and African-American) works that broached this issue rather comprehensively are Richard Wright's *Native Son* and Ralph Ellison's *Invisible Man*. These novels chart the lives of quite different protagonists, but both ponder the same essential questions regarding black male survival. Is it, in fact, possible for the black man to thrive in a society that has predicated its very survival on the subjugation of this same black man? And if he can thrive, what strategies must he adopt to do so? What is the role of the black woman in this struggle?

While both novels end pessimistically, they anticipate the novels of Ernest J. Gaines, who, from his *Catherine Carmier* (1964) to *A Lesson Before Dying* (1993), has focused almost exclusively on the plight of the black man, using his Louisiana settings as a locus for America as a whole. Gaines does not shy away from the harsh realities of black male existence, willingly confronting episodes of violence and psychological encroachment, yet he still offers hope for continued survival, acknowledging, of course, that the black male's survival in the past is a testament to his future endurance. Gaines's novels present in fictionalized form prime examples of the different techniques that black men use to cope and survive. *The Men of Brewster Place* also comments on such strategies.

Naylor addresses in varied ways the insults historically leveled against African-American dignity, but she also takes the African-American community to task on its own oppressive tendencies. Challenging African Americans' willingness to transform themselves from the "oppressed to the oppressor," Naylor unabashedly confronts the community's attitude on sexual orientation. In some instances the topic is presented overtly; in others it is treated simply as a given. An entire chapter in *The Women of Brewster Place* is devoted to a lesbian relationship and the difficulties Theresa and Lorraine face as they try to fashion a life together. *The Men of Brewster Place* acknowledges the sexual confusion of Eugene Turner as he wrestles with impending realization of his homosexuality. In *Linden Hills* Winston Alcott abandons his partner David of eight years in order to honor his family's expectation of marriage. Even though Winston is ashamed of his decision, he feels obliged to hide his sexuality in order to ensure his success in upward mobility and material acquisition. *Bailey's Cafe* presents the issue rather matter-of-factly. Jesse Bell is introduced as a married woman who maintains a lesbian relationship as though her tendencies are as "normal" as those of anyone else. While it is clear that Naylor's particular treatment of homosexuality is yet another example of her insistence on expanding boundaries, and reconsidering notions of centeredness and normalcy, her attention to this topic also disputes African-American innocence. That is, by offering examples of African-American infraction, Naylor prevents a complete recentering of African-American identity. She cannot simply challenge "whiteness" as the standard and then replace it with "blackness" as the new righteous social core. African-American culpability in homophobic offense keeps the Postmodern center forever in flux, and coerces all human beings, black, white, or otherwise, to interrogate their perspectives continually.

Naylor has enjoyed both critical acclaim and widespread popularity since the "Lucielia Louise Turner" chapter from *The Women of Brewster Place* was first published as a short story in *Essence* magazine in 1980. Her public appeal is largely the result of early access to both *Essence* and *Redbook*. While *Essence*, with a circulation of just under one million, is targeted mainly to middle-class African-American women readers (though it also boasts a substantial black male readership), *Redbook*, with a circulation of over five million, attracts young white married women and mothers. Following the 1980 publication, *Essence* published the "Kiswana Browne" chapter from *Women* in 1982. Then in late 1988 *Redbook* reprinted the "Mattie Michael" chapter from *Women* in anticipation of the March 1989 television premiere of the film version of *The Women of Brewster Place*. As a result of these efforts, Naylor has been a mainstay in American literature and popular culture from the beginning of her career.

It is clear that the cause of her broad appeal is twofold. On the one hand, her style is simple and is thus accessible, yet she writes with such emotional and intellectual depth that she does not insult her reader. On the other hand, her ability to transcend race in regard to her readership is due primarily to her skill at making African-American issues generic human (or human rights) issues. Consequently, both black and white women respond favorably to Naylor's sensitivity and compassion for her characters.

Like the popular response the critical response has been praiseworthy. In a 1982 review for the *New York Times* Annie Gottlieb writes of *The Women of Brewster Place*: "Miss Naylor bravely risks sentimentality and melodrama to write her compassion and outrage large, and she pulls it off triumphantly." And commenting on *Linden Hills* in 1985, also for the *New York Times*, Michiko Kakutani comments, "[O]ne is quickly beguiled by the actual novel—so gracefully does Miss Naylor fuse together the epic and the naturalistic, the magical and the real." Bharati Mukherjee, writing for the *New York Times* in 1988 on *Mama Day*, insists that "Gloria Naylor has written a big, strong, dense, admirable novel; spacious, sometimes a little drafty like all public monuments, designed to last and intended for many levels of use." A *Publishers Weekly* reviewer in 1992 states that the "beauty of Naylor's prose [in *Bailey's Cafe*] is its plainness, and the secret power of her third novel is that she does not simply tell a story but brings you face to face with human beings living through the complexity, pain, and mystery of real life," and a 1998 *Publishers Weekly* reviewer applauds *The Men of Brewster Place* and Naylor for "neatly bind[ing] the stories' themes together . . . and . . . offer[ing] readers a grace note of optimism that is as credible as it is moving." Naylor's novels address issues and embrace themes that have concerned not only the African-American literary tradition, but also African-American cultural/racial experiences. Without question, she will continue to favor her readers with works that challenge, delight, and enlighten and that encourage intellectual exploration and critique.

3

The Women of Brewster Place
(1982)

Described on the cover as "a novel in seven stories," *The Women of Brewster Place* chronicles the lives of seven black women as they struggle to survive in a rapidly deteriorating neighborhood. Most of the women have arrived at the title setting as a result of influences beyond their control. The wall at the end of the street that prevents through traffic serves as a reminder that their lives here are restricted in ways that even they do not fully understand. As is true of her later novels, Naylor disregards the traditional linear structure. Instead of depending on a singular, easily measurable, plot development, Naylor uses several miniplots that highlight the lives of the individual women. In this way, Naylor focuses more directly on characterization than on narrative movement. She still spins an entertaining tale; her methods are less traditional but more compelling.

PLOT DEVELOPMENT

Each individual woman's story provides the basis for a minimal plot. The novel opens with the story of Mattie Michael and how she came to live at Brewster Place. Mattie's story also lays the foundation for some of the themes later developed in other chapters. As this first chapter begins, Mattie, forlorn and seemingly friendless, is moving to Brewster

Place. Still somewhat shaken about why she has had to move, Mattie begins to reminisce and to chart the steps of her life that have led to this moment. The bulk of this chapter, then, is narrated via flashback. Covering a thirty-year period from the 1940s to the 1970s, this chapter tells of Mattie's fall from grace and of her inability to forgive herself and lay the past to rest. The chapter opens in the 1970s, but as soon as Mattie begins to recall the past, the time period shifts to the 1940s. For the duration of the chapter, Mattie's story is told chronologically, the chapter returning ultimately to the 1970s.

When Mattie is twenty and still living with her parents in rural Tennessee, she is seduced by notorious womanizer Butch Fuller. Soon finding herself pregnant, she confides in her parents, Sam and Fannie, but fearing a potentially violent reaction, she refuses to reveal to her father, "an old man with set and exacting ways" (19), the identity of the baby's father. Realizing that she cannot make peace with her father, Mattie leaves home on the bus and travels east, soon arriving in a no-name city where her childhood friend Etta Mae Johnson resides.

After the baby (named Basil because he was conceived in an herb garden) arrives, Mattie struggles to work and care for him. Etta Mae, the eternal wanderer, leaves town once she is confident that Mattie and Basil are fine. Mattie soon discovers, however, that living in her present squalid circumstance is more than she can bear. Her frustrations intensify when she is startled one night from her sleep by the piercing screams of Basil who has been bitten by a rat. Deciding that she can no longer live in this place, Mattie packs up Basil and wanders the street in search of more suitable accommodations. Finding none and becoming increasingly tired and confused, Mattie finds herself lost and on the verge of tears.

Just as she is about to give up all hope, Mattie, lugging Basil through a strange neighborhood, is accosted by an equally strange woman. Mattie soon discovers, however, that the old woman, Miss Eva Turner, is a godsend. After learning of Mattie's troubles, Miss Eva invites Mattie and Basil into her home, initially to rest and eat, but for the next thirty years, Mattie and Basil will live in Miss Eva's house. A crafty old lady, both warm and ornery, Miss Eva refuses to accept payment from Mattie, telling Mattie instead to save her money, insisting that Mattie is doing her a favor by being good company while Basil serves as a compatible playmate for Miss Eva's granddaughter Ciel, who also lives there. The two women run a fairly harmonious household; tensions mount only when Miss Eva suggests to Mattie that she is overprotective of Basil and implies that Mattie may live to regret these actions, whereupon Mattie always threatens to leave but never does.

A few years after Mattie and Basil move in, Miss Eva dies. And because Mattie has saved all the money that she would have spent on rent, she buys the house so that Basil will always have a place to live. After Ciel's parents reclaim her, only Mattie and Basil are left. And without Miss Eva's balancing discipline, Mattie spoils Basil incessantly so that by the time Basil is thirty, he has no sense of responsibility to himself, his mother, or society.

Basil soon finds himself accused of manslaughter, the result of a barroom brawl, and instead of letting him remain in jail until his trial as her attorney suggests, Mattie posts bail after offering up her house as collateral. Initially grateful to his mother, evidenced in his willingness to assist with household chores or to chauffeur his mother around town, Basil ultimately sours at the thought of having to endure a trial, even though the attorney assures both Basil and Mattie that Basil will be exonerated. Just days before he is to appear in court, Basil flees. Consequently, Mattie loses her house and is relegated to live in Brewster Place.

The second chapter presents the escapades of Etta Mae Johnson, Mattie Michael's childhood friend from Tennessee. As this story opens, Etta is returning to Brewster Place, this time from Florida where she has stolen the car of her most recent paramour. When Mattie warns Etta that she is certainly being pursued by the law for stealing the man's car keys, Etta, in inimitable Etta fashion, presents Mattie with a pair of men's monogrammed underwear, stating, "I'd have to be a damned good pickpocket to get away with all this" (58). Completely unfazed by her own actions, Etta is always in pursuit of the next opportunity. Unlike Mattie, Etta leads life in the fast lane, and though she, like Mattie, is now in her fifties, Etta, to Mattie's consternation, refuses to slow her pace and "act her age."

Just hours after her arrival, Etta, at Mattie's behest, reluctantly accompanies Mattie to church for evening services. Mattie hopes to encourage Etta to consider settling down, perhaps even finding a suitable mate among the church members. However, Etta sets her sights on the minister, Rev. Moreland T. Woods. Increasingly consumed with the possibilities of a life with a man like Woods, Etta begins to fantasize about being a preacher's wife and finally garnering for herself the respectability that such a role affords. Of course, Etta is concerned more about the messenger than about the message. It is the Reverend's style that excites

Etta, one that Etta "had encountered . . . in poolrooms, nightclubs, grimy second-floor insurance offices, numbers dens, and on a dozen street corners" (66).

While Etta has been sizing up the Reverend, he, too, has been estimating her body, noting that she "was still dripping with the juices of a full-fleshed life" (67). Instantly, he decides that he must meet her, in much the same way that Etta has set her sights on him. Insisting that Mattie introduce her to Reverend Woods after the service, Etta coquettishly follows Mattie toward the pulpit where Etta and the Reverend engage in a game of cat and mouse. Quickly understanding the game that is afoot, Mattie quietly cautions Etta to be careful, a show of concern that Etta mistakenly takes as a critique of her inadequacy to become the next Mrs. Woods. Mattie then realizes that, yet again, she must allow Etta to make her own mistakes and simply remain the true friend she has always been, picking up the broken pieces of Etta's heart once this imminent fiasco has run its course.

The minister invites Etta out for a cup of coffee whereupon Mattie returns home to await Etta's later return. Just as Mattie predicted, Reverend Woods wants Etta for only one purpose—sexual release. Finding herself later that evening in a cheap motel with Woods, Etta is forced to shatter the fantasy in which she allowed herself to wallow for a few hours. Ashamed of herself for thinking that she could outsmart a con artist like the Reverend, Etta returns to Mattie's apartment defeated and tired. Nevertheless, Mattie awaits the arrival of her friend without a word of condemnation; instead, she offers only love and consolation.

The third chapter offers a topic and characters that differ from those in the first two chapters. Instead of focusing on women who have been mistreated by men, the next story depicts a young woman who, though legally defined as an adult, must live several more years before she can even begin to understand what being a mature woman entails. Kiswana (née Melanie) Browne is a twenty-three-year-old rebel manqué, eclipsed by any real revolution by at least five years. Still determined to find her cause, this would-be activist is one of three characters (the others are Theresa and Lorraine who appear in the sixth chapter) who live in Brewster Place by choice. Kiswana comes from a privileged middle-class family in Linden Hills (the upwardly mobile black community not far from Brewster Place and also the title setting of Naylor's second novel).

As the story opens, Kiswana is sitting by the front window in her sixth-floor apartment daydreaming about imaginary tenants in the throes of escaping down fire escapes from an inferno. Her creative juices are flow-ing unheeded when suddenly Kiswana notices her mother's fast approach to her building. Snatched from her mental wanderings, Kiswana must quickly prepare her apartment for her mother's first, and unannounced, visit, a task made more burdensome by the fact that Kiswana is certain her mother will hate the apartment and the neighborhood.

In a climactic moment in the chapter, Mrs. Browne must correct Kiswana's misguided notions about what Kiswana calls the Browne's "terminal case of middle-class amnesia" (85). Mrs. Browne assures Kiswana that she and Kiswana's father are as concerned about the poor as Kiswana is, though they do not need to live in Brewster Place to prove themselves. She cautions Kiswana that the long-awaited revolution will not materialize because society has moved to another phase. Instead, she admonishes Kiswana to work within the system by becoming an assemblywoman or a civil liberties lawyer or by opening a freedom school in the neighborhood. She provides Kiswana with various ways of using her talents instead of allowing them to waste away in dead-end jobs. Being a practical thinker, Mrs. Browne tries to provide Kiswana with a practical means of employing her radical ideas so that they yield some good. By the end of the chapter, Kiswana understands and appreciates her mother a bit more, though she is still reluctant to admit this truth.

The fourth chapter finds an adult Ciel (Miss Eva's granddaughter) struggling to keep her common-law marriage intact and to maintain a semblance of a family life with "husband" Eugene and her baby daughter Serena. Throughout the course of their relationship Eugene has periodically abandoned his family, but this time when he returns, Ciel hopes that he will stay. Even though Mattie, now surrogate mother to Ciel, is skeptical that Eugene will fulfill his familial obligations, Ciel believes, tentatively at least, that he will stay. And all seems to progress rather smoothly—that is, until Ciel discovers that she is pregnant once again.

Soon she notices a transformation in Eugene. For weeks prior, he has come home from work and eagerly assisted in chores around the apartment, even painting and sprucing up the place a bit. But now that Ciel is pregnant, Eugene becomes sullen, distant, and mean. Ultimately he blames Ciel for their economic straits, and even though she offers to secure outside employment (still a problem since Eugene does not want Mattie caring for Serena), Eugene balks, bemoaning the fact that he will never get ahead with Ciel and babies only burdening him.

Finally believing that she has no alternative (if she wishes to salvage her marriage), Ciel terminates her pregnancy, and though the abortion causes her emotional strife, she willingly accepts the pain as long as Eugene remains in Brewster Place. Her optimism is short-lived, however, for soon after the abortion, Eugene comes home to announce that he has accepted a job in another state. As Ciel begins to question him on the details of this sudden decision, she finds inconsistencies in his story. Finally he tells her that he simply must go, but that he will send for her and Serena in a few months. Realizing that her supplications are going unheeded, Ciel seeks out her daughter for comfort at which exact time Ciel hears screams emanating from the kitchen.

While Ciel and Eugene have been arguing, Serena has been engaged in a hide-and-seek game with a roach. When the roach seeks safety in an electrical socket, Serena attempts to retrieve her new playmate with the tines of a fork, only to be electrocuted instantly. Ciel now finds herself all alone, grieving not only for Serena but also for the baby whom she lost trying to please Eugene. Lapsing into the deepest depression, Ciel, completely oblivious to her surroundings, tries to will herself to die in order to stop the pain. Upon realizing Ciel's intentions, Mattie rushes to Ciel's rescue in what is one of the most moving scenes in the novel. Carefully easing a frail (physically and emotionally) Ciel out of bed, Mattie places her in the bathtub, and using only her bare hands, proceeds to bathe Ciel in a symbolically charged scene. The ritual bathing not only cleanses Ciel's body but also redeems her spirit.

In a unique structural twist, Naylor opens this story ostensibly at the end. As the chapter begins, Eugene, engaged in conversation with Ben, the building superintendent and neighborhood drunk, complains that he is misunderstood and mistreated. And as a consequence, he will not attend Serena's funeral. Because he has been banned from any association with Ciel (by Mattie and other friends), Eugene refuses to pay his respects if he cannot "be there . . . with [his] woman in the limo and all, sittin' up there, doin' it right" (90). Eugene's misguided male ego prevents him from honoring his responsibilities not just as a father, but as a human being. And although Eugene thinks he deserves a certain amount of respect, it is painfully apparent that he has not commanded respect in his most recent actions. He represents the kind of perverted manhood against which these women must try to function.

In the fifth chapter Naylor engages in a psychological critique of the title character, Cora Lee. A stereotypical tenant in this downtrodden neighborhood, Cora Lee is the single mother of seven children, most of whom have different fathers. From even the earliest moments in her own childhood, Cora Lee has been fascinated with babies. However, once they mature beyond infancy, she has little use for them. Cora Lee's only concerns in the present moment are the care of the latest baby, which she performs with an almost religious zeal, and her daily attention to soap operas. Living in a fantasy world, Cora Lee has become inured to the squalor of her everyday existence. Only when the outside world intrudes upon her sanctuary (in the form of a disgruntled neighbor who threatens to call the police on Cora Lee's undisciplined children, or in the form of an unruly child who has injured himself and requires medical attention) does Cora Lee suspend her fantasy life, but only to dispense with the unwelcome encroachment as quickly as possible.

On one of these fantasy-laden days, Kiswana intrudes on Cora Lee's world to alert the irresponsible mother to the fact that one of her sons has been riffling through the garbage in search of food. Completely unfazed, Cora Lee is perturbed more by the interruption than by the information. Quickly understanding that these children need some kind of intervention, Kiswana pursues a protracted dialogue with Cora Lee so that she can observe more closely Cora Lee and her children.

After a few strained moments (with Cora Lee itching to return to her soap operas), Kiswana, ultimately deciding that the children need an outlet for their youthful energy and a cultural experience to satisfy their innate curiosity, invites Cora Lee to bring them to an Afrocentric performance of Shakespeare's *A Midsummer Night's Dream*, an adaptation for which Kiswana's director boyfriend Abshu has secured a city grant. Initially, Cora Lee balks, fearful that the children, in their inability to comprehend, will embarrass her. However, Kiswana soon convinces her that the play has been adapted to suit and entertain children.

On the night of the performance, Cora Lee is surprised at the response of her children. Enamored with what they see, one of the sons even asks if Shakespeare is black, a question to which Cora Lee, in an effort to encourage his enthusiasm, offers, "Not yet" (127). During the fleeting moments when the play is being staged, Cora Lee engages in her own dream. For the first time since entering motherhood Cora Lee is consumed with new possibilities for her children, considering that they might even go to college. After all, Cora Lee's own brother and sister are firmly entrenched in the middle class, her sister even owning a house in Linden Hills. This cultural experience broadens Cora Lee's perspective. Instead of saying, "I just don't know" (a comment that Cora Lee repeats throughout the chapter regardless of the topic at hand), Cora Lee thinks about not only what she can know but also what the children might come to know if their energies are channeled in a productive direction.

Unfortunately, just as the play must end, so does Cora Lee's emergent transformation. After returning home and putting the children to bed, Cora Lee welcomes the nocturnal visit of yet another shadow (the narrative reference for the nameless men with whom Cora Lee engages in sexual activity). Cora Lee's life returns to business as usual; once again she rejects her own promise and that of her children in trying to foster a better existence. While many of the other women in the text can attribute their hardships to the machinations of men, Cora Lee willingly allows herself to be used, ultimately deciding that she would rather live in a fatherless and husbandless house than suffer physical brutality at the hands of a would-be spouse, as if those are the only two alternatives.

While most of the previous chapters have focused on men's oppression of women, the sixth chapter is concerned with women's oppression of other women, in this case heterosexual women's prejudice against lesbians. Here Naylor examines the concept of "the oppressed becoming the oppressor," and what seems to be the need of all human beings to feel better than someone else.

Lorraine and Theresa are a lesbian couple who have moved to Brewster Place to escape possible persecution from residents of the more affluent neighborhoods where they can certainly afford to live. Lorraine, a timid and unassuming elementary school teacher, fears the wrath of her students' parents if she is discovered to be a lesbian. And though Theresa, a personnel director at the board of education, is unfazed about the opinion of others, she moves to what she considers a godforsaken part of town to allay Lorraine's apprehension. Nevertheless, within days of their arrival, gossip ensues and once again Lorraine begins to question the wisdom of this most recent move.

While the other women in the neighborhood are initially skeptical of Lorraine and Tee because of their youth and attractiveness and because of the possibility that the women's husbands and boyfriends might show interest in the two newcomers, they soon breathe a sigh of relief when they notice Lorraine's and Theresa's indifference to the men. But after the women's suspicions mount, their skepticism turns to muted anger once they determine that Lorraine's and Theresa's "friendly indifference [is simply] an insult to the women [and] a brazen flaunting of unnatural ways" (131).

Because the residents need proof for their suspicions, they appoint

Sophie, gossipmonger, busybody, and closest neighbor to the couple, as watchdog, a responsibility that she assumes with an almost religious zeal. Riffling through garbage or trying to peek into the women's shopping bags when they pass by, Sophie searches for any telltale sign of indiscretion. When Ben, building superintendent and resident alcoholic, returns from the couple's apartment after making a minor repair, Sophie interrogates him, and even after he assures her that he witnessed only the horrors of a broken faucet, she, needing to imagine some evil-laden ritual, questions why they need to use so much water.

Sophie's illogic exemplifies the continued idiocy that plagues the couple's lives. Such a constant bombardment eventually takes a toll on their relationship. When Lorraine first mentions to Theresa that the other women are no longer friendly, Theresa immediately launches a verbal attack, stating to Lorraine that she need not broach this subject, because if Lorraine is leading up to a suggestion of moving again, she can simply abandon the thought. Quickly Lorraine is reminded that Theresa, sullen and detached, does not seek the approval or acceptance of people in the way that Lorraine does, and as a consequence Theresa is completely unconcerned about the thoughts, suspicions, or homophobic fears of her neighbors. Lorraine, on the other hand, yearns to trade makeup secrets and recipes with the other women. More gregarious than Theresa, she needs external validation.

Determined to secure herself a place in Brewster, Lorraine decides to become involved in the block association that Kiswana is trying to establish. Offering her services as association secretary, Lorraine is summarily rejected when Sophie begins to question the integrity of the appointment, given, at least in Sophie's opinion, Lorraine's moral degradation. When a heated discussion between Sophie and Etta (who rises to Lorraine's defense) ensues, Lorraine rushes from the room visibly shaken, having confronted in its ultimate form the unbridled cruelty of human ignorance. Finding her efforts in forming a bond thwarted, Lorraine is left feeling alienated from and abused by the human chain. And fearing an "I told you so" from Theresa, she is left with no one to console her. Or so it seems.

Following on her heels after her abrupt departure is Ben, who offers Lorraine both comfort and sanctuary, inviting her to his humble but clean hovel of an apartment in the basement. Forging a bond with the most unlikely of residents, Lorraine soon learns that Ben has also been abandoned and rejected by society. That they are two human beings is enough for Ben and Lorraine to foster a friendship that offers each of them comfort and renewed hope. Social status gives way to emotional need as they replenish for each other the well of compassion, commitment, and consideration.

While the kindness that Ben bestows upon Lorraine is due in part to his amiable nature, he is also trying to right a wrong that has plagued him for a while. Several years earlier Ben and his former wife Elvira worked as sharecroppers in rural Tennessee, along with their slightly crippled (and unnamed) daughter. On weekends the daughter performed housework for the landowner Mr. Clyde, who insisted that she stay overnight. Ultimately, the daughter relates to Ben and Elvira that she is being molested, and though Ben wants to question Mr. Clyde about the accusation, Elvira cautions him not to, angrily criticizing Ben for believing the daughter, for not providing the family with better circumstances, and for being a poor excuse of a man.

Unable to cope with his wife's shrewish ways, yet unable to avenge the offense against his daughter, Ben begins to drink heavily as a means of numbing his emotional pain. Now, living in Brewster Place, he still needs intoxication in order to keep the ghosts of the past at bay. However, when he meets Lorraine, he is reminded of his helpless daughter, and the pain from his sharecropping days resurfaces. Still, he wants to protect Lorraine as a means of redeeming his past inaction in regard to his daughter. Consequently, he informs Lorraine that she is welcome to visit him at any time.

On one fateful evening Lorraine decides to go to a nightclub without Theresa, a previously unheard-of act. Upon returning to the Brewster neighborhood, Lorraine is accosted and then brutally raped by C. C. Baker, the neighborhood gang leader, and his minions, who then leave her in an alley to die. Early the next morning Ben staggers into the alley on his way home to sleep off one of his binges, when he suddenly sees Lorraine sprawled on the ground, bloody and disheveled. When he approaches her, Lorraine, now completely disoriented, starts attacking him with a brick, ultimately bludgeoning him to death, not only ending her relationship with Theresa and her life in Brewster Place, but also snuffing out her chances for continued emotional growth.

The seventh and final chapter of the novel is narrated as a dream. Mattie Michael dreams about a neighborhood block party that the tenants' association is sponsoring in order to raise money for a lawyer. At Kiswana's urging, the association has decided to threaten the landlord with a suit if he refuses to make certain environmental improvements. The chapter serves as a finale to the previous chapters. Ciel even returns in this chapter, happier and more self-assured than she has ever been. Announcing that she now lives in San Francisco and that she is engaged, she expresses to Mattie her appreciation for all that Mattie tried to do for her during her bereavement. The scene also witnesses Etta, to Mattie's consternation, vigorously trying to retain her youth, dancing to the music with the energy and animation of a teenager. Unfortunately, this chapter also finds Cora Lee pregnant yet again and still ignoring her older children. Nevertheless, it is Cora Lee who prompts the women's final defiant gesture, which serves as the climactic ending to the chapter and to the novel. Upon noticing a blood spot on the wall at the end of the street, Cora Lee calls to the other women that "It ain't right; it just ain't right. It shouldn't still be here" (185), at which point the women proceed to dismantle the wall brick by brick. And even though a rainstorm ensues, the women remain steadfast in their effort to remove not only the bloody bricks, but also the imprisoning wall that has kept them trapped in so many ways. Even Theresa assists in the effort though she is still burdened by recent events with Lorraine.

Just before the chapter ends, Mattie wakes from her dream, a narrative development that reminds the reader that recent events are mere imaginings. Nonetheless, the novel still ends with hope. In the final words of the text, Etta calls up to Mattie from outside, "Woman, you still in bed? Don't you know what day it is? We're gonna have a party" (189). Obviously, then, the women are taking matters into their own hands, determined to remove—slowly, methodically, and consistently—the various obstacles that have impeded their progress in life.

CHARACTER DEVELOPMENT

Even though the overall structure of the novel allows the reader only a mere sketch of the lives of the women, Naylor still does a convincing job of developing her characters completely. While each woman is showcased in her own individual chapter, some of them also appear in other chapters. And with each appearance the reader is afforded yet another insight into the particular identity of the character.

The one character whose presence unifies the text is Mattie Michael, as she appears more often than any other character, and she is developed more fully than all others. Appearing in Etta's story, in Ciel's story, in Cora Lee's story, in "The Two" chapter, and in "The Block Party" chapter, Mattie serves the function of surrogate mother and spiritual guide.

Nonjudgmental in her approach, Mattie understands completely her role as friend and confidante to others. While she realizes that Etta Mae is once again hurling herself into disaster, Mattie knows she cannot stop her. She can only be there for her "to pick up the pieces when it's all over" (70). Because she has learned from her own mistakes with Butch Fuller and with her son Basil, Mattie understands that people with the best intentions sometimes make the most egregious errors. And though she was abandoned by Butch and by her own father (in his reaction to her pregnancy), Mattie is determined to support those in her life, even when they err. Though Mattie is equipped with a sustaining compassion for others, she is not perfect, as is evident in her emotional scars. While Mattie has accepted the loss of her house at the hands of Basil, and has accepted her fate in Brewster Place, she refuses to discuss the circumstances that have led to her move. Indeed, she is a woman who offers comfort to others, but she is still a human being who suffers quietly with her own psychological pain.

Mattie's greatest service is done for the adult Ciel, granddaughter of Miss Eva. When Ciel's daughter Serena dies suddenly, and only days after Ciel is compelled by her "husband" to have an abortion, Ciel also seems to die. Upon realizing that Ciel intends to will herself to death, Mattie rushes to the rescue. Because she understands women's emotional lives, with the attendant frustrations and disappointments, Mattie is sensitive to Ciel's plight. Her past experiences have afforded her insight, if not into Ciel's immediate circumstances then certainly into the depths of Ciel's pain. It is important to note as well that the Ciel chapter, according to Naylor, spawned the entire novel, not the Mattie Michael chapter as readers often think.

To some degree when Mattie saves Ciel, she also saves herself, and the ritual bathing that she performs on Ciel becomes a testament to the healing powers of sisterly love and bonding, particularly in the face of a chauvinistic, male-centered world. Mattie, then, becomes a catalyst for possible change. And though to some degree Mattie wallows in the past (when she refuses to discuss her life with Basil, or when she refuses ever to seek the love of a man), when she "baptizes" Ciel, Mattie is also cleansing her own spirit and forgiving herself for her past indiscretions.

Mattie's ultimate contribution to the story, however, is her willingness to think through certain controversial issues and, without falling victim to irrational outbursts, offer a reasonable assessment of the circumstances. Such behavior is best exemplified in a crucial conversation between Mattie and Etta Mae. Discussing their concerns/reservations about the lesbian couple, Mattie and Etta strive to be fair and open-minded as they embark upon an intellectual critique of the gay couple. That they are willing to expend such energy is to their credit. And when Mattie finally states that perhaps the emotional bond the lesbians feels for each other is not radically different from the emotional bond of two longtime friends like Etta Mae and Mattie, she reveals a notable level of intellectual and emotional development. To be sure, she has made significant strides from her fundamentalist rural Tennessee beginnings, symbolized in the behavior of her father upon learning of her pregnancy. Instead of judging, Mattie struggles to understand.

That Mattie Michael is a central character is made evident in the last chapter, "The Block Party," wherein the story is told in a dream sequence, Mattie's dream. Since Naylor chose Mattie to have a dream about hope and the future, the reader must acknowledge Mattie's significance and her relative transformation from one who seems stagnant (as she wallows in the past) to one who emerges as a vehicle for change in the other women.

Because Etta serves as a foil character (one who highlights the qualities of another character by contrast and/or similarity) to Mattie and as a dynamic character (one who exhibits psychological, emotional, and/or intellectual depth), Etta is also significant in Mattie's development. Never shying away from fun or from confrontation, Etta has always challenged the status quo, whether that meant defying white authority in the 1930s' South or simply ignoring social mores in the present day. In her unrestrained lust for life she seems to be very much in control of her destiny. However, Etta also divulges an emotional vulnerability (thus, depth) in her interaction with Reverend Woods. In the past Etta was always confident and self-assured, and although she spent much of her early life chasing dreams and men, she seemed oblivious to validation from men. Nevertheless, when she actually ponders the possibility of marrying Woods, she reveals a yearning to be respectable and middle-class. Such desire exposes an emotional capacity that both softens and humanizes Etta.

Second to Mattie, in terms of character development and frequency of appearance, is Kiswana Browne, the young woman who lives at Brewster Place by choice. Perhaps because she is the youngest of the seven main characters she has the greatest potential for growth and change. Though somewhat naive, Kiswana, with her energy and focus, is determined to improve the lives of the Brewster Place tenants. And while her initial strategies may seem flighty to more seasoned and practical minds, Kiswana is to be commended for her tenacity and for her sensitivity to those less economically privileged than she.

A college dropout (not from a lack of ability, but of motivation and focus), Kiswana has spent the past several months assuming one job after another only to find herself unemployed yet again. She has now decided to save the tenants of Brewster Place by organizing the residents to rally against their uncaring slumlord. While her effort is commendable, her unwieldy sense of righteousness is misguided. Oftentimes, Kiswana's expectations are not grounded in reality; rather, she allows her imagination to run unchecked. Soon she will discover, however, that an untamed imagination and an untempered ego can prove to be a volatile combination.

Kiswana is challenged by her mother to put her talents to good use. Her mother would prefer that Kiswana return to college and pursue a lucrative career, although Mrs. Browne realizes that such will not occur. Instead, then, she encourages her daughter to fulfill her wishes to improve the conditions of Brewster Place, but by working within the social/political system, not by haphazardly criticizing it. Described as "a tall copper-skinned woman" (76), Mrs. Browne moves with a confident stride. Clearly, she is a woman who has lived long and experienced much, and when she and her daughter clash, it is obvious that the mother emerges as victor because her genuine sense of self infuses her with poise and correctness. Although Kiswana sees her mother as only a bourgeois (plagued by superficial middle-class values) imitation white woman who has abandoned her roots, Mrs. Browne is simply a product of civil rights successes and a sheer determination to fight for and then accept the fruits of her labors. While Kiswana rebukes her parents' success in an effort to prove how sympathetic she is to the plight of the poor, Mrs. Browne identifies her personal success as an example of the rewards that any black person can achieve. For Kiswana, capitalist successes define what is wrong with society; for Mrs. Browne, they define the infinite possibilities for all.

Kiswana does not want to admit the validity of her mother's comments because in doing so she would be tacitly acknowledging her mother's intelligence, a gesture that would completely alter the dynamics of their relationship and would force Kiswana to see herself differently. For so long she has defined herself in opposition to her mother, but now she must view herself in alliance with her mother. As the narrative reveals, "She . . . suddenly realized that her mother had trod through the same universe that she herself was now traveling" (87).

Kiswana's further development is highlighted in "The Two" chapter when she hosts a block association meeting. Taking her mother's words to heart, Kiswana has found a practical solution to some of the community's problems. By convincing the residents to band together, Kiswana realizes that as a unified group they can challenge the slumlord more forcefully and perhaps make some inroad toward improvement. And by the end of the novel, within Mattie's dream and in the postdream conclusion, the community has rallied together to raise funds to hire an attorney so that their demands are heard within the system, just as Mrs. Browne suggested to Kiswana earlier in the story. That she ultimately listens to her mother, while still maintaining her core desires, serves as a testament to Kiswana's growth, not only as an activist but also as a mature woman.

Besides Mattie, Etta, and Kiswana, of the seven main characters, the other women who exhibit a notable level of change are Lorraine and Theresa. As the narrative charts their relationship, the reader witnesses role reversals for the two characters. Interestingly enough, after Lorraine starts visiting with Ben, she gains a level of confidence that she has never before exhibited. Even Theresa notices certain changes; Lorraine now speaks up for herself, and she no longer defers to Theresa's opinion as often as she once did. And though Theresa has always wanted a more forceful Lorraine, she is still perturbed that an alcoholic Ben is able to do for Lorraine in a few days what Theresa has not done in a few years. And as Lorraine's strengths become more pronounced, Theresa's vulnerabilities emerge, and latent tensions in their relationship mount.

Their heated debates about the role of sexual orientation in defining one's identity provide some of the most compelling scenes in the novel. And as a means of making them both dynamic characters, Naylor showcases the validity of both women's point of view. Lorraine believes that she should not have to live in a world where her every move is suspect simply because she is a lesbian (after all, she asserts, on the day after she discovered she was a lesbian she was no different than she was on the day before). Yet Theresa argues that they, as lesbians, are very different, mainly because those who define difference are the ones who are in power: socially, politically, and economically. Each woman is correct in her assessment. Lorraine simply speaks from the perspective of the individual (lesbian), while Theresa argues with the acknowledgment that the individual is still susceptible to society's standards, right or wrong. These two characters' development is shaped by the intensity of their commitment to their respective beliefs.

The only male character significantly developed is building superintendent Ben. While one might initially dismiss Ben as a wayward drunk,
the reader soon discovers that Ben is possessed of a human depth that
surpasses the would-be humanity of many of the women. Once the
reader is made privy to Ben's former life, she or he better understands
Ben's present circumstances. Had Ben been given a fair chance in life,
he might have turned out differently. But when he fails (either by inaction or by social oppression) to protect his daughter, he loses his sense
of manhood, succumbing instead to a weaker form of self. He is an
alcoholic in the present moment because he does not want to remember
the circumstances that brought him to this point. In an ironic twist, then,
Ben's drunkenness (a seemingly unmanly, weak act) is the result of his
wanting so desperately to be a man and to forget his inability to be such.
Perhaps in his intoxication, he can fantasize about being a fully realized
man. On the day of Serena's funeral, in conversation with Eugene who
cannot bring himself to attend because he wants to avoid the wrath of
the women (as their wrath would diminish his manhood), Ben echoes
Eugene's sentiment: "Yeah, a man's gotta be a man" (90). Immediately
after, the narrative reveals, "Ben felt the need to wet his reply with another sip" (90). That Ben would speak of manhood in tandem with taking
another sip of alcohol supports this point.

Significant minor characters include Miss Eva, the busybody Sophie,
and Ben's wife Elvira. Miss Eva serves not only as a surrogate mother
to Mattie when she welcomes Mattie and the baby Basil into her home
but also as a foil character to Mattie. When Miss Eva sees Mattie coddling
Basil and excusing his mischievous ways, she warns Mattie to be stricter
with him, warning Mattie that if she places all of her energies on Basil,
she will have nothing left for herself. Of course, her words will ultimately
ring true. Miss Eva serves, as well, as a contrast to Mattie in regard to
her feelings for men. While Mattie has decided to forgo men for the
remainder of her life, Miss Eva, though much older, still has a healthy
regard for the opposite sex, revealing to Mattie that she likes all men,
regardless of physical attributes. And though Miss Eva encourages Mattie to pursue a relationship with someone, Mattie demurs, stating instead
that her only concern is in raising Basil. When the adult Basil betrays
Mattie at the end of the first chapter, Miss Eva, though now dead,
through her prophecy and wisdom lives on and maintains an important
place in the novel.

An equally important minor character, Sophie serves as resident gossipmonger and hypocrite. She assumes a self-righteous air, but Sophie is

not quite as religious and God-fearing as she would have the community to believe. In the sixth chapter, "The Two," Sophie, assuming a pseudo-Christian posture, challenges Lorraine's and Theresa's right to live in Brewster Place, suggesting that she wishes to protect the moral integrity of the neighborhood. However, the reader recalls the narrative introduction to Sophie, albeit brief and subtle, in Cora Lee's (the fifth) chapter. In this chapter, Sophie yells obscenities up and down the corridor about Cora Lee's unruly children. To be sure, Sophie is a fickle character who serves to remind the reader of the danger of extreme behaviors. Antagonistic in her approach, Sophie forces the other characters and the reader to defend their more reasonable positions.

More despicable than Sophie in her minor role is Ben's wife Elvira, whose insensitivity and unchecked selfishness serve, ironically, to balance the scales of female goodness/victimization versus male evil that the novel seems to uphold. That a mother would ignore the pleas for intervention of a crippled daughter regularly molested is beyond rational thought. And when Elvira exacerbates the problem by attacking Ben's manhood (suggesting that if he were half a man, he would have given her more babies instead of this useless disabled daughter), she becomes, ironically, for the reader a catalyst for empathy with the plight of black men like Ben. With the Elvira and Ben story, the reader is alerted to the fact that the larger Brewster community, regardless of gender, is susceptible to the machinations of a racist, class-struck society. As with all significant minor characters, Elvira adds a dimension to the intellectual discussion that would otherwise be lost.

THEMATIC ISSUES

The Women of Brewster Place critiques the concept of human survival in all of its manifestations: the strategies human beings adopt to survive, the mistakes made, and the lessons learned. As part of this investigation, the novel focuses in part on parent-child relationships. Because parents want so desperately for their children to enjoy a life better than the one they have endured (in the face of racism, economic oppression, and/or political machination), they often overindulge their children materially or overprotect them in compensation for voids imposed by society. When Sam Michael discovers that daughter Mattie is pregnant, he is highly disappointed in part because he had cherished such high hopes for her and in part because he blames himself for having protected her so tightly from interaction with other young people, especially boys. He believes that Mattie succumbed so easily to physical temptation because she had been allowed practically no latitude for social interaction. Racked with guilt, Sam thinks now that he should have been more lenient with Mattie. The added irony to this particular story is that Mattie, responding to her own upbringing, becomes too lenient as a mother and, as a result, helps to create a disastrous situation with an adult Basil. Partly in defiance of her father (she must prove that she can survive without his authority) and partly in need to prove something to herself, Mattie sacrifices herself, effacing her complete identity, in exchange for Basil's welfare: in short, she spoils him miserably. Both Sam and Mattie sacrifice for the betterment of their children, but their efforts go awry.

Human survival is also addressed thematically by highlighting the oftentimes stifling effects of the past on the present. So often characters are waylaid by life circumstances that all but stunt their continued emotional growth. Mattie is stunted sexually because she refuses to seek the love of a man, mainly because she feels guilty for her past action. Instead of forgiving herself and moving to fulfill herself with other opportunities, Mattie snuffs out any hope of a rewarding marriage or relationship. Rather, these energies are devoted solely to Basil. Likewise, Ben, wallowing in despair and guilt about the wrongs done to his daughter, allows the past to sap any possibility for growth and change. Even Kiswana, in her zeal to fight a revolutionary war in the interest of black people, lives in a past replete with Afros, raised fists, and marches. Her mother informs her that while those former efforts yielded some good, it is now time to employ different strategies instead of waiting for a revolution that will never occur. Mrs. Browne insists that Kiswana dispense with issues that, in Mrs. Browne's estimation, are no longer relevant. In a conversation about the definition of blackness, Mrs. Browne alerts Kiswana to the fact that blackness has no specific criteria, that Kiswana is no blacker for living in Brewster Place and the Brownes are no less black for living in Linden Hills. Mrs. Browne, quite proud of her heritage, insists that "black isn't beautiful and it isn't ugly—black is! It's not kinky hair and it's not straight hair—it just is" (86). To limit blackness to a narrow definition, according to Mrs. Browne, is to live in the past.

The concept of collective support, or interdependence, functions as the ultimate theme to be developed. Instead of individuals struggling to survive alone or instead of allowing the past to circumscribe even their modest efforts, by the end of the novel, key characters are working together in a countermaneuver against the various obstacles that impede their progress. And even though this theme is pursued in a dream sequence, the narrative point is clear: inroads into societal improvement are made more easily and more permanently with communal support. When the women decide to dismantle the wall at the end of their dead-end street, they are working collectively to liberate themselves, both physically and mentally. Ironically it is Cora Lee, seemingly the least likely to initiate any positive change, who begins removing the bricks. Formerly passive and rather complaisant, she now feels equipped to take action as a result of the bond forged among the women.

The issue of racism is presented in the novel, but it does not take center stage. Since the informed reader is well aware of its pervasiveness, Naylor resists the temptation to overexpose race. And to some degree, she preserves for her characters some sense of agency. Had Naylor made race a major focal point, she would have run the risk of objectifying and thus perverting the characters. That these economically disadvantaged blacks live on a dead-end street within a stone's throw of a major thriving thoroughfare is proof enough of the prevalence of institutionalized racism. But instead of focusing on the sources of such bias, Naylor attends to the black response to these circumstances. Again, black resistance and survival (mere survival is an act of resistance) are the focus.

HISTORICAL CONTEXT

The novel spans the thirty-year period from the early 1940s (the time of Basil's birth) to the mid-1970s (upon Ben's death), a time of significant political and social change for African Americans. The post-World War II period witnessed the second Great Migration . . . (the movement of African Americans from the rural South to the urban North in the hope of gaining economic advancement while escaping bigotry and violence; the first Migration had occurred following World War I). Scores of blacks left the South to seek employment in northern factories and to benefit from the postwar economic boom. While looking to the North as some kind of Promised Land, many blacks became disheartened by the squalid conditions they found there. Urban poverty was more pronounced than the conditions they had known in the South where even under the sharecropping system, they could plant and grow food. Moreover, blacks found that their living arrangements were just as circumscribed as they were in the South. Even if they could afford better circumstances, they were denied access. Or as blacks moved into certain areas, whites soon moved elsewhere, and these abandoned neighborhoods, without a sub-stantial tax base because jobs and economic prosperity followed the whites to suburbia, soon deteriorated to slums. When the Supreme Court rendered its decision in *Brown v. Board of Education* (1954), the modern Civil Rights Movement was ushered in, but years would pass before any significant inroads toward social equality would be made. Even after the Civil Rights Act of 1964 and the passage of the Voting Rights Bill of 1965, poor African Americans, in both the North and the South, found their conditions largely unchanged.

It is within this social context that Gloria Naylor writes *The Women of Brewster Place*. Described as "the bastard child of several clandestine meetings" (1), Brewster Place originated, soon after World War I, as a locus for the oppression of already oppressed people. Shoddy materials were used in the erection of buildings, while mismanagement and ne-glect completed the task of dehumanization. Naylor reminds the reader of this economic reality when she describes the wall that blocks off Brew-ster Place from a major thoroughfare. Clearly, Naylor suggests that the lifeblood of the neighborhood has been stanched, and the inhabitants have been left to fend for themselves or to die. Most die, if not physically, then emotionally, because the coping skills they have cultivated were designed for a more agrarian existence with its emphasis on open spaces, nature, and the solace offered in extended families. Many of the char-acters hail from the South. For Ben, Mattie, Etta Mae, and Ciel, Tennessee is their place of origin; for Theresa, Georgia. And though each of them has come to the North for different reasons, each has come to escape some perceived ill in their southern environs. The irony, of course, rests in the fact that their present conditions have brought new ills.

As a means of counteracting some of these problems, Naylor advances the philosophy of certain characters, and in so doing, nods to a signifi-cant literary development: the Black Arts Movement of the 1960s and early 1970s. Coalescing in 1965, soon after the assassination of Malcolm X, it insisted upon "social engagement" (the sustained and pointed cri-tique of the white establishment) as a prerequisite of its aesthetic func-tion. This movement disregarded white literary forms and perceived white sensibility. In short, the Movement challenged white mainstream notions of good, normal, and standard, much like Equiano does in his slave narrative. (See Literary Heritage chapter.) Black power (if neces-sary, armed self-defense) and pride in black identity were staples of the organization. Kiswana Browne, though somewhat misguided in her zeal, emerges as the representative of this movement. Arguing with her mother that the family (her mother, father, and brother) has acquiesced willingly to white notions of superiority, Kiswana espouses a revolutionary agenda, even though Mrs. Browne reminds Kiswana that all of her former college "revolution" friends are now a part of the establishment. Naylor, however, uses Kiswana to voice some important concepts, radical though they may be, about black racial pride, lest they be forgotten. Kiswana's boyfriend, Abshu, maintaining only a minor role, also embodies the best of revolutionary ideals at work. Instead of merely protesting and ridiculing social norms, he is involved in reshaping the community and advancing the intellectual and artistic capacity of the residents. It is his Afrocentric (using African-inspired costumes, language, and humor) rendition of Shakespeare's *A Midsummer Night's Dream* that Kiswana takes Cora Lee's children to see. As a result of his efforts, children in the community are exposed to art forms they otherwise might never see. And he imbues these productions with black identity so that the children can relate to the art.

Perhaps Naylor's most radical use of the often radical Black Arts Movement is evident in Lorraine and Theresa, and ironically so. Frequently criticized as homophobic and chauvinistic, the Black Arts Movement often relegated women to an inferior status and either ignored the contributions of gays or denigrated them for being emasculated, willingly, by a sexually perverse white establishment. Naylor, however, invokes the spirit of the Movement in her development of these two lesbian characters, and in so doing, makes them mouthpieces for the Movement. Each woman argues from a different perspective, but each is quite radical in her assessment. Lorraine, initially shy and unassuming, wants to be accepted for who she is, insisting that the larger community see her as being no different from other women/people there. After all, she maintains, she is no different today than she was on the day before she realized she was/is a lesbian. On the other hand, argues Theresa, the world, homophobic and heterosexist as it is, is ruled (in sheer numbers) by persons who despise gays and lesbians. And while Theresa could not care less what others think, she realizes that she must function in a world controlled by others. Each woman is quite passionate in her appraisal, and with this passion, each woman plants the novel firmly in the tradition of Black Arts radicalism.

NARRATIVE STRUCTURE

Naylor's reluctance to adopt a linear structure in this first novel anticipates what will become a recurring technique in her other novels. The author enjoys testing the boundaries of reality while exploring various possibilities for the imagination. A more fluid structure allows her latitude to present all these possibilities. While each story in *The Women of Brewster Place* is captivating in its own right, and each story is only tangentially connected to any other story, Naylor still provides an overall unity that sustains the novel.

The Women of Brewster Place shows in poignant detail the detrimental effects of men's emotional and physical violence on women, and in more subtle detail the ill effects of racism on black lives. Nevertheless, these potential victims are determined to survive despite their inhuman treatment in a world that would rather see them demonized and defeated. The women's repeated attempts at resilience culminate in a final chapter of communal resolve when they decide to demolish the wall at the end of the block in a symbolic move to reject the machinations of men and whites to keep them caged, both metaphorically and in actuality.

Each story/chapter is presented by a third-person omniscient narrator. An omniscient narrator, in addition to providing details about the action in a story, knows the thoughts and feelings of the characters and reveals this information to the reader. As stated above, the novel does not tell one specific story; rather it tells several distinct stories. Nonetheless, Naylor still manages to craft a cohesive work that moves toward a recognizable resolution. The unity is maintained with the recurring appearances of key characters in various stories. Because the novel opens with the Mattie Michael story, the reader automatically embraces Mattie as the protagonist. Capitalizing on this response, while still creating enough narrative space for other characters, Naylor uses Mattie in the other stories as a unifying thread.

The chapters are also connected thematically. Issues discussed in one chapter are presented in later chapters, though in altered forms. For example, the "Mattie Michael" chapter, in addition to other issues presented, focuses in part on dysfunctional parent-child relationships. Later, in the "Cora Lee" chapter, this topic is rendered more perversely. Cora Lee reproduces incessantly, only to ignore the children once they pass infancy. Her obsession is with newborns, and once she can no longer nourish them directly from her body, she abandons them emotionally, and they are left to fend for themselves.

NARRATIVE TECHNIQUE

Though defined as a novel, *The Women of Brewster Place* comprises seven distinct stories/chapters. This structure underscores Naylor's thematic and character components. In the individual stories, each woman is presented with her own unique personality, one that is finely crafted so that she is both memorable and forceful. Each chapter is complete in terms of the character sketch and plot movement. There is a discernible conflict and a resolution, at least temporarily, of that conflict. Even though Mattie Michael, for example, never forgives herself for past mistakes (and thus her chapter might seem incomplete because of a lack of closure), she has reconciled herself to her present circumstances and moves forward with her life, which is evident in her rescue of Ciel. By having each woman involved in what becomes a complete story, Naylor showcases the fact that inasmuch as black women's lives, particularly during this period, are fraught with frustrations and painful moments, these same lives are punctuated with minor victories that ultimately lead to a life well lived. Each story reveals a moment, or a few moments, in time when the women arrive at a new revelation, one that will redirect them on a slightly different path. Without this narrative technique, the novel would perhaps lapse into a sketchy hodge-podge that merely exploits the woes of weak victims.

Inasmuch as the work must be considered in light of the individual stories, one must still attend to the novel as a whole. Each woman is an integral part of a cohesive group whose success or failure as an interdependent body depends on the collective efforts of its members. Naylor convincingly echoes this fact by placing certain characters in recurring roles. The interdependent nature of the relationships is highlighted in the casual way that the characters impact each other's lives. For example, Mattie Michael appears in the "Etta Mae" chapter to salve Etta's emotional scars and to provide hope. She appears again in Ciel's chapter for the same purpose. Kiswana Browne, after yielding to some of her mother's advice in her own chapter, serves as a role model in the "Cora Lee" and "The Two" chapters. Likewise, Etta Mae, who has risen from the defeat suffered in her own chapter, advances as a voice of reason in

"The Two" chapter. In their recurring roles, these women reveal how even the slightest action taken can have a definite impact on another life. And the reciprocal interactions create a strong bond among the women that becomes their most vital weapon when, at the end of the novel, they combine their efforts to dismantle the political and social impediments to their success.

Naylor also relies on key images or concepts to connect the various chapters. In this way, each life story, while maintaining its unique quality, functions in relation to another life story. For example, at the beginning of Mattie's chapter, when she is moving into Brewster Place, the moving van is described as creeping along "like a huge green slug" (7). Then, at the beginning of the next chapter, Etta Mae's method of transportation, an "apple-green Cadillac," is described as moving "like a greased cobra" (56). From these descriptions the reader learns that both women are threatened by a slow-moving, yet methodical and deliberate nemesis. The concept of spirituality, or reverence, also serves as a connecting vehicle. When Mattie, in a baptism ritual, bathes Ciel back to health, her action is ironically linked to Sophie's maintaining a "religious vigil" (131) over Lorraine's and Theresa's apartment, or to Cora Lee's "reverently" (107) handling her newborns or "religiously" (112) dusting and mopping their sleeping areas. It is with these subtle links that Naylor makes her most impressive aesthetic gestures. As different as each of these women may be, there is still maintained an ineradicable bond.

A FEMINIST READING

Feminist criticism has emerged out of an effort to identify, expose, and then dismantle (or deconstruct) the various ways women are excluded, exploited, suppressed, and oppressed. Feminist critics examine images of women in literature by both women and men in an effort to challenge the representations of women as "other," as less than or inferior to men. The critics, who themselves can be women or men, question literature's perpetuation of stereotypes about women. They ponder, for example, whether women and men are essentially different biologically or if they are socially constructed as different. For instance, the feminist critic, whose very political and social critique considers all fixed definitions of identity as tools of a dominant patriarchal structure, would be quick to point out that, even as society tries to define a man as strong, aggressive, and focused and a woman as passive, compassionate, and sensitive, examples abound that undermine this assessment: sensitive men and self-assured, demanding women. Feminist criticism asks, then, "What is a woman?" or "What is feminine?" and more importantly, "Who is crafting the definition and for what sociopolitical purpose?"

Some feminist criticism may examine language and its collusion in the attempted dehumanization of women. Or it may assess the role of social institutions in the continued breach of individual women's rights. Feminist criticism may also investigate the function of race, class, and general social standing in one's exploited circumstance. In short, the feminist critic examines power relations in texts in order to expose such relations in life with the intent of razing patriarchal structures of inequality. For the feminist, reading (and critiquing) is always a political act.

Clearly, *The Women of Brewster Place* provides a perfect model for exploring some of the concepts of feminist theory and criticism. In every chapter, Naylor addresses women's sexuality and questions the role of this sexuality in defining the person/woman. Mattie Michael snuffs out her sexuality and is thus defined by sexual denial. Etta Mae is defined by sexual pursuit (she equates sex with love and never finds a suitable mate). Miss Eva has enjoyed many men, but only within the confines of marriage; hers is a healthy regard for sexuality, because she has always retained sexual control over her life. Sex has caused Ciel to suffer because the result of the sexual encounter, her children, have been taken from her. Cora Lee abuses sex, accepting little or no responsibility for introducing more babies into the world. Kiswana is in the throes of sexual awakening in her relationship with Abshu, and, in a process of maturity, she also begins to see her mother as a woman, a sexual being. Lorraine and Theresa are defined only by their sexuality, as though society can define them only as one-dimensional creatures because they are lesbian, or perhaps society defines all women in this way, but because Lorraine and Theresa are ostensibly untouchable (the rape of Lorraine notwithstanding), they are cast away as perverse other. Even Ben's unnamed daughter learns early on that as a woman, she might well be victimized because of her gender; consequently, she opts for a life of prostitution, rather than suffering at the hands of sharecropping landowner Mr. Clyde, so that she can have a measure of control over her life.

That women are defined (and then either accepted or rejected) by their ability to serve in the sexual gratification of men is made evident in the scene of Lorraine's rape by C. C. and his gang. To highlight the phallocentric world that women must try to function and survive in, the narrative voice in "The Two" offers the following description of the gang:

"These young men wouldn't be called upon to thrust a bayonet into an Asian farmer, target a torpedo, scatter their iron seed from a B-52 into the wound of the earth, point a finger to move a nation, or stick a pole into the moon—and they knew it. They only had that three-hundred-foot alley to serve them as stateroom, armored tank, and executioner's chamber. So Lorraine found herself, on her knees, surrounded by the most dangerous species in existence—human males with an erection to validate in a world that was only six feet wide" (170).

Every description in the previous passage is sexual in nature. Clearly, Naylor is turning the tables as she defines men by their sexuality, suggesting that every action in which they engage is, in some way, indicative of their need to expose their sexual energy. Every social institution established, every political maneuver executed, every economic takeover performed is man's effort to showcase virility. Feminist criticism affords the reader language such as "phallocentric" to describe a world in which male genitalia serves as a kind of god to be worshiped, especially since its every move determines the fate of everyone within its reach.

Still, there is another important component to this description. Naylor confines all men to the role of sexual predator. At this juncture race, class, and social status as distinct entities collapse, as all women become grouped together in an antagonistic stance against all men. Though C. C. Baker and his gang are to be despised for their actions, Naylor is careful not to place their dehumanized nature only on black men, or poor men. She reminds the reader that the most "civilized" of European men must act out the same fantasies. The only difference is that they have the resources and the power to execute their desires. Even an action supposedly as patriotic as planting a pole on the moon is presented/construed as suspect. No male power, then, is left unaffected by the depictions illustrated here.

4

Linden Hills
(1985)

While *The Women of Brewster Place* (1982) addressed, for the most part, the plight of black women in a poverty-stricken, and seemingly hopeless, community, *Linden Hills* critiques the burdens and misguided notions of a well-established, upwardly mobile black community. And though Naylor maintains her focus on the especial frustrations of the black woman, she broadens her approach and also details the psychological pains of the black man. Continuing with her signature style, Naylor relies upon the story cycle to structure the novel. *Linden Hills*, then, is composed of several stories, and because Naylor models the novel after a section of Dante's epic poem *The Divine Comedy*, the stories accommodate, in number, the various levels (and stories) highlighted in Dante's "Inferno" section. With this novel, Naylor begins to take more stylistic and narrative risks, strategies that she will continue to hone in the later novels.

Linden Hills details the various ways in which blacks have exchanged their souls for even the slightest chance to enjoy an improved material life. Naylor questions the extent to which these characters have in fact lost their blackness or, at the very least, that essential part of their individual personalities that makes them unique. With unflagging criticism, Naylor challenges the various forms of elitism, homophobia, chauvinism, intraracial bias (color prejudice within the black community), and the like, which plague a community so desperately trying to be acceptable to the larger white community. In an ironic twist, Naylor creates characters who profess their desire for a solid black community but who in reality shun blackness and snuff out any emergent sign of its development.

PLOT DEVELOPMENT

Instead of creating a clearly defined plot, in her typical fashion Naylor all but abandons plot in favor of theme, character development, and narrative manipulation. However, to maintain narrative interest, Naylor, adopts the miniplot, as she did in her first novel. *Linden Hills*, then, is composed of several ministories wherein Naylor explores questions about the black middle class and critiques the misguided value system of that community.

Main characters Willie Mason and Lester Tilson, twenty-year-old amateur poets, spend five days in December walking through Linden Hills seeking work at odd jobs to earn money for Christmas gifts. As they proceed through the community, they encounter residents who maintain quietly distressed lives while attempting to appear happy and fulfilled. Lester, who ironically lives in Linden Hills, serves as guide for Willie in an effort to prove to Willie that life in this upscale neighborhood is fraught with despair, pain, spiritlessness. Willie, who hails from the lower-class Putney Wayne community, observes not only with awe-stricken wonder the apparent spiritual void of Linden Hills but also with relative pride the accomplishments of these same citizens in creating lives free of the economic insecurity that has forever plagued his own life.

As the two continue on their journey, Willie will ponder his own existence and begin to question, with anticipated regret, his former decision to abandon high school prior to graduation. Periodically throughout the novel, Willie challenges Lester, who has been afforded more advantages than has Willie, to re-think his negative opinion about Linden Hills. It is this journey, then, that holds together the structure of the novel. In short, the discoveries attained by both men provide the only plot movement. The standard plot question of "what will happen next?" becomes "what will they discover next?"

In addition to the plot movement provided by Willie and Lester's journey, Naylor employs yet another journey that serves as subplot. Willa Prescott Nedeed, the wife of Linden Hills' most prominent citizen Luther Nedeed, has been locked in the basement of the Nedeed home, along with her five-year-old son Sinclair, for several weeks because her husband believes that someone else fathered the boy. Just days before Willie and Lester begin working in Linden Hills, Sinclair dies, leaving Willa to mourn and to harbor hatred for Luther.

The Willie/Lester narrative is interspersed with excerpts from Willa's life in the basement with her son's corpse. While thus incarcerated, Willa, riffling through old trunks and boxes, discovers the letters, cookbooks, diaries, and other possessions of the Nedeed women who preceded her. In reviewing these materials, Willa learns that these wives and mothers had to suffer emotional hardships when they sacrificed their own happiness for the betterment of the Nedeed legacy. In the course of her reading, particularly over the five days of the Willie/Lester journey, Willa finds peace when she realizes that each of her predecessors, in rejecting the status of victim, found a means of emotional survival, whether it was perfecting recipes, maintaining a journal, or merely reveling in her own beauty. Willa decides that she, too, must regain a measure of control over her life. The plot questions for this narrative become "will she attain such control?" and "how will she reincorporate herself into the Nedeed family?"

The Linden Hills neighborhood is designed such that the farther down the hill one proceeds the more affluent the residents. Lester and Willie are moving in this direction. At the very bottom of the neighborhood is the Nedeed house, situated at the end of a private drive and detached from the other houses on prestigious Tupelo Drive. The Nedeeds have owned the land in Linden Hills for over 160 years, since 1820. The original Luther Nedeed (the direct line of Nedeeds were all named Luther), upon purchasing the land, envisioned the construction of an affluent black community, and all of its would-be inhabitants would have to support that same vision: upward mobility, family values, and a conservative sense of black unity. All residents were financed through the Nedeed-owned Tupelo Realty Corporation, which leased the land to prospective home buyers for 1,000 years with the stipulation that if any Nedeed/Tupelo criteria were defied, the land would revert to the corporation. Every Luther Nedeed, or every generation, prided himself on maintaining this vision and legacy, not the least of which was marrying a woman who supported the same vision and who honored the Nedeed name by reproducing a dark-skinned male heir. Willa Nedeed made the unforgivable error of producing a light-complexioned son.

The dysfunction of the present-day Nedeed household represents the generic tensions of the larger Linden Hills community. To some degree, the farther down Lester and Willie journey and the richer the residents are, the more heightened these tensions become. Before the two men begin their five-day work marathon, they visit their two closest friends, a married couple who in fact suggest that they seek work in Linden Hills. Ruth and Norman are financially strapped as are Willie and Lester; their presence in the novel serves as sharp contrast to the other minor characters whom Willie and Lester will encounter. A former Linden Hills resident, Ruth abandoned those roots for her husband, and while it might be both financially and emotionally feasible for her to return to Linden, she does not. Norman is plagued with an emotional disorder that prevents him from maintaining a job for any measurable length of time. Every two years, usually for three months, he suffers from hallucinations that result in his mutilating his body because he thinks he sees pink organisms overtaking his skin. For over six years, Ruth has remained committed to Norman despite the financial burden and realization that they may never enjoy a better life. The Ruth/Norman ministory preserves a level of humanity that seems lost in Linden Hills. While those residents sacrifice all for financial stability and social status, Ruth sacrifices the latter for her love of Norman. And even though she has told herself to leave every year, she honors her vows and remains. Ruth and Norman's six-year marriage serves as a foil to Luther and Willa's. Just because Luther suspects that his wife has been unfaithful, he endangers her life and allows a child to die, whereas Ruth, whose material life is in shambles, remains constant in her devotion. Even when Norman promises Ruth that they will live one day in Linden Hills, Ruth replies that she will never go back there. Each of the poor characters, Lester, Willie, Norman, and Ruth, are presented as more humane, more compassionate than are the wealthy.

Lester and Willie's first job involves cleaning up on the occasion of the social event of the season: the wedding of one of Linden Hills' most eligible bachelors, Winston Alcott. The two are to work in the kitchen and stay clear of the reception party, but they steal moments to observe the behaviors of the wedding party and the bourgeois guests. To Lester and Willie, these blacks are not real; instead, they seem mechanical, stilted, and artificial, fearful that if they laugh too heartily, they might be misconstrued as lower-class people. Everything seems quite unnatural to Lester and Willie, a feeling substantiated when they realize that what has just been passed off as a marriage ceremony is, in fact, a farce. For the best man's toast, David paraphrases a Walt Whitman poem that expresses homoerotic emotions. Willie, analyzing the subtext of the toast, discovers that Winston and David are, in fact, lovers and that David is indicating his dismay at what he considers a fake marriage. This exchange clarifies for Willie, and for Lester once Willie explains, that survival in Linden Hills requires people to lie not only to others, but also to themselves; residents must sacrifice a part of their souls (their natural selves) in order to be accepted in this community. Later, the novel reveals that it was, indeed, Luther Nedeed who orchestrated this entire fiasco when he anonymously alerted Winston Alcott's father that his son just might be gay, threatening as well to forward incriminating evidence should the matter be ignored. Willie and Lester are not privy to this information, although the third-person narrative reveals to the reader Luther's collusion in this affair. And although Winston loves David and wants to share a life with him, he thinks his greater duty is to uphold the traditions of the community, which entail maintaining a heterosexual family and producing offspring.

While there are several ministories strategically placed throughout the novel, the other significant one highlights the frustrations of Laurel Johnson Dumont whose story also serves as a link, albeit tenuous, to the Ruth Anderson and Willa Prescott Nedeed stories. Laurel's is the only story that encompasses her whole life, roughly from age four to her mid-thirties. It is the story of a woman who fulfilled practically every childhood dream, only to discover that dreams realized so easily transform into nightmares. Like many of the other characters, Laurel has lost her essence in favor of material gain. As a child Laurel spent her summers in rural Georgia with her paternal grandmother Roberta Johnson, who while exacting in her ways generally acquiesced to Laurel's every wish. When, at age five, Laurel refuses to steer clear of a water-filled ditch, Roberta provides the girl with swimming lessons. And when Laurel grows up to become a champion swimmer and even wins a scholarship to Berkeley for synchronized swimming, Roberta cashes in her life insurance policy to pay tuition even though she despises everything about the state of California. And when Laurel, at thirty-four, seems to be wasting away in depression (her marriage to Howard is failing, and she is no longer fulfilled in her executive position at IBM), Roberta, now eighty, travels all the way to Linden Hills to rescue, yet again, her granddaughter.

Roberta arrives in mid-December, several days before Lester and Willie begin their journey throughout the neighborhood. After some coaxing Laurel tries to revive some holiday spirit if not for herself, then at least for Roberta. Deciding to call her only two friends, Ruth and Willa, Laurel sets out to put her house in order. Thinking a renewed sister-bond with these women can salvage her rapidly deteriorating emotional state, Roberta is determined to cook and decorate her way back to normalcy. But when she cannot locate Willa (the reader knows that Willa is locked in her basement) and when an ill Ruth cannot visit, Laurel succumbs once again to depression. Her condition worsens when Luther Nedeed alerts her to the fact that since her husband has filed for divorce and has vacated the premises, since they have no children, and since the land was originally leased to the Dumonts, she must leave as well. For Laurel, her whole adult life in Linden Hills has been a complete farce. The anxiety she has felt about her very existence grows deeper, and she relinquishes her hold in a final act of suicide. On a snow-laden December day Laurel dives headfirst into her empty Olympic-size pool while Lester and Willie are shoveling snow in her front yard. Laurel's tragic end exposes the potential horrors that await anyone who lives in Linden Hills.

Finally, on Christmas Eve Willie and Lester descend to the Nedeed estate to assist Luther in holiday preparations. Having explained that his wife and son are away visiting relatives, Luther indicates to the two men that he would like to enjoy some holiday cheer in their absence. Willie, visibly shaken whenever in Luther's presence, voices reservations about accepting the task, but Lester insists that they fulfill their obligation, especially since Luther has agreed to double whatever they have earned at the other houses.

Lester and Willie are asked to assist Luther in decorating the tree with various family heirlooms. The men are surprised to discover that a man as strange as Luther would be this sentimental, but for Luther, anything associated with the Nedeed name is to be admired if not completely worshiped. While the three men are busy dressing the tree, Willa is downstairs making preparations to return upstairs and to put her life back in order, even if she must break down the door leading to the basement. In this final chapter the main plot and the subplot converge when Willie, completely unaware, unlatches this door and thus gives Willa access once again to the house. Throughout the novel, Willa has been a nameless and practically faceless character. Not until minutes before she emerges is she named, a narrative ploy that would suggest her return to the main house is also a reclamation of identity. Prior to ascending the basement stairs, Willa furiously cleans the downstairs area and fully intends to do likewise in the other areas of the house, in an effort to cleanse their lives of all past wrongs while reestablishing herself as Mrs. Luther Nedeed. It is her simple attempt to regain the power of choice in her life.

But once she enters the house carrying her son's corpse, everything goes awry. Luther, after dismissing Willie and Lester, defiantly attempts to block Willa's path, a gesture that she takes as a challenge; consequently, she strikes out at Luther. During this struggle the lace material covering the corpse catches an ember in the fireplace, and quickly the three bodies—Luther's, Willa's, and Sinclair's—are consumed in an inferno that ultimately destroys the house. Willie and Lester look on with horror, initially at the roaring fire, but then at the windows of other houses on Tupelo Drive where residents just watch the house burn without offering the least bit of assistance. The novel ends with Willie and Lester left to ponder what has just occurred, and they are left with the ultimate task of deciding how to conduct their own lives.

CHARACTER DEVELOPMENT

In *Linden Hills* four characters are developed more fully than all others: Lester, Willie, Laurel, and Willa. The reader witnesses most events from the perspective of Willie and Lester. Their changing opinions during their five-day trek through the neighborhood provide ample opportunity for the reader to observe their relative growth and maturity.

Both Willie and Lester disdain everything about Linden Hills, from its bourgeois mores to its pristine lawns. As a true outsider, living in the nearby Putney Wayne community, Willie, also a junior high school dropout, believes that anyone living in Linden Hills looks down on him and considers him less than human. As a consequence, he has conducted his life in complete opposition to everything that Linden Hills represents. Instead of embracing the principles of upward mobility, which include proudly gaining a formal education, Willie has rejected even a modicum of success—his ability to read at a junior high level. Willie believes that to participate in the dreams espoused by Linden Hills is tantamount to effecting one's own intellectual and psychological death. Refusing to document his own poetic creations by writing them down, Willie instead commits them to memory in an effort to preserve the purity of his thoughts. For him, "the written word dulls the mind, and since most of what's written is by white men, it's positively poisonous" (29). And since Willie considers Linden Hills a live minstrel show (in this case, white

American attitudes presented in "black" face), it, and all it represents, is "positively poisonous."

Lester's disgust with Linden Hills stems from a personal conflict. As a resident of the neighborhood, he is supposed to shoulder the responsibility of preserving the unwritten tenets of the community. But at age twenty, Lester finds achieving success, Linden Hills–style, at best daunting, at worst completely impossible. Soured by the fact that he watched his father drive himself to an early grave in an attempt to provide the family with a confirmed middle-class standing, Lester is determined to follow a different path. Or at the very least, he is determined to make his mother, who wants Lester to be more aggressive and take initiative, suffer in her embarrassment for Lester, mainly because he blames her and her social demands for his father's untimely death. In short, Lester's lack of initiative is grounded in part by a determined rebellion. While criticizing his Linden Hills neighbors for losing their souls, Lester tries to excuse himself from achieving success and independence, implying that if he were to accomplish some goals, he might risk becoming yet another resident devoid of spiritual or intellectual substance.

Willie and Lester serve as mentors for each other, helping each other along in their discoveries about Linden Hills and in their self-discoveries. Early in the novel Willie tries to convince Lester that perhaps life in Linden Hills is not as detrimental as Lester would argue it is. On the night before he and Lester begin their journey through the neighborhood in search of work, Willie spends the night at Lester's house, which he shares with his mother Mrs. Tilson and sister Roxanne. And because he has never enjoyed such a comfortable living environment, Willie, in a sudden appreciation of African-American material success, softens his attitude about Mrs. Tilson and the neighborhood in general. When Lester scoffs at Willie's slight transformation, Willie reminds him that, in all of his condemnation of Linden Hills, he has not chosen to leave. For all of his ostensible disgust with the people and the neighborhood, Lester still harbors some respect for what they have achieved. By the end of the novel, Lester's self-righteous attitude has subsided significantly. And much later in the novel, just prior to the climactic end, when Willie balks at the idea of working for Luther Nedeed, Lester, in a moment of maturity, urges Willie to honor his promise to fulfill this last work obligation. And though Willie still feels ill at ease in Luther's presence, he, at the very least, is awed by Luther's achievements. Throughout the novel one may observe scenes in which these two assist each other in their emotional development. In this regard they serve as foil characters for each other, one always supplying the strength or push when the other is lacking. This sustained brotherhood provides the brief resolution presented at the end: "Each with his own thoughts, they approached the chain fence. . . . Hand anchored to hand, one helped the other to scale the open links" (304).

It is vitally important that they have come to appreciate their interdependence by the end of the novel, because without the strength and support of the other, neither would cope as easily as they will now with the cataclysmic climax, the destruction of the Nedeed estate. When they realize that the Nedeed house is burning, and with Luther, Willa, and Sinclair inside, they attempt to alert nearby Tupelo Drive neighbors, all of whom ignore the repeated requests for assistance. Helplessly watching the house burn to complete destruction, Willie and Lester are dumbfounded at what they have just witnessed: the total abandonment and inhumanity of Linden Hills residents in regard to the Nedeed plight. In several of the last lines of the novel, both a stunned Lester and a baffled Willie repeat, "They let it burn" (304). Neither will fully understand the reaction (or lack of reaction) of the neighbors, whether they are rebuking Luther specifically, or whether their Linden Hills–sponsored inhumanity has gotten the better of them. As a result, both men will feel some responsibility for the future of the neighborhood, and each of them has developed enough to realize their new roles.

Willa Prescott Nedeed's development is easily charted in her narrative movement from victim (or object) to agent (or subject). Early in the novel, even before she is formally introduced, Willa is presented as a suffering victim in a most horrific circumstance. On at least two occasions prior to beginning their search for work, Willie and Lester overhear what seems to be the plaintive wail of an injured animal echoing from the depths of Linden Hills. Not until later does the reader realize that it was Willa Nedeed's cries upon discovering the untimely death of her son, some days after she and he are forcefully banned to the basement. But as her subtextual narrative develops, Willa emerges, not as an object to be shuttled about at Luther's whim but as a willing and capable agent determined to control her own fate. Willa's growth is brought about in part by her daily ritual of "reading" (interpreting) the lives of three of the Nedeed wives who preceded her. Scanning the letters of one, the recipe ledgers of another, and the photographic journal of yet another, Willa comes to understand that perhaps she has not suffered nearly as much as these other women, yet somehow they cultivated enough strength and resolve to survive the emotional assaults leveled by their respective Luther Nedeed. For example, Luwana Packerville Nedeed married the first Luther Nedeed in 1837 only to discover that she was also his slave, that in fact he had purchased her and that she had absolutely no rights as a free woman. Her days are spent writing imaginary letters to an imaginary sister she also names Luwana. Nevertheless, in writing to herself and engaging in introspection, she manages to remain relatively stable. And then there is Evelyn Creton Nedeed who, according to the narrator, "must have been a bewildered woman." In order to cope she is "[d]riven by the need to spend so much time in that kitchen. To be sure that she never ran out of ingredients for the excuse to keep large round bowls between her thighs and long wooden spoons in her hand all day" (188), Evelyn always maintained a stockpile of supplies. Or in the case of Priscilla McGuire Nedeed, survival means reconstructing her role in life once her former role is denied to her. When Willa initially begins perusing Priscilla's photo album, the early pictures (always of Priscilla, husband Luther, and son Luther—the men are always named Luther) suggest a charmed life for the woman. As the son ages and grows in each successive photograph, Priscilla becomes less and less noticeable. As the narrator finally observes, Priscilla "was no longer recording the growth of a child; the only thing growing in these pictures was her absence" (209). As a result, Priscilla pursues gardening, focusing her attention on the growth of plants instead of the growth of her son.

In "reading" these stories Willa ultimately emerges as a composite of these three women. She takes their stories and makes them her own, but like her namesake Willie, Willa does not record any of her thoughts. She preserves them for herself as tools to assist her in preparing for her future: "No, she could no longer blame Luther. Willa now marveled at the beauty and simplicity of something so small it had lived unrecognized within her for most of her life. She gained strength and a sense of power from its possession. . . . She was sitting there now, filthy, cold, and hungry, because she, Willa Prescott Nedeed, had walked down twelve concrete steps. And since that was the truth . . . whenever she was good and ready, she could walk back up" (280). It is with this renewed sense of determination that Willa does in fact mount the steps, with her dead son in her arms, and attempts a return to her life as Mrs. Luther Nedeed. That she dies at the end, along with Luther and son Sinclair, is less significant (at least when considering only Willa) than is her transformation from beginning to end, as one who formerly saw herself as helpless but who ultimately sees herself as capable indeed.

Laurel Dumont's story, as highlighted in the Plot Development section, serves as a tragic reminder that material success is not always accompanied by happiness. But this character is developed to shed light on other narrative concerns as well. For one, Laurel's story serves as contrast for Willa Nedeed's story. As the reader learns during Laurel's tale, Laurel and Willa, prior to the novel's opening, had formed a friendship, not an equal sisterhood per se, but one whereby Willa seemed awestruck by Laurel's confidence, poise, and sheer independence in the face of all odds. And Laurel enjoyed the fact that she was the envy of the unofficial first lady of Linden Hills. However, as the novel reveals, each woman's life would take a different turn. Even though both will die by novel's end, it is Laurel who falters in her struggle while Willa ascends, both literally and figuratively, the steps toward redeeming herself and shedding the weak persona that formerly identified her. In addition, Laurel's story helps to foreground the theme of fragmentation. As Linden Hills resident historian Daniel Braithwaite, in a brief analysis of Laurel's suicide, suggests to Willie and Lester, "[T]hat personal tragedy today was just a minute part of a greater tragedy that has afflicted this community for decades" (257), a community, also according to Braithwaite, "as broken and disjointed—as faceless—as Laurel Dumont's body" (261). Laurel's confusion, then, underscores the increased confusion, for the past thirty or so years, of Linden Hills residents who have aspired to attain a black power without white encroachment, only to discover that to sustain their community even minimally, most of them would have to enter the white world and, ironically, invite (if only unwittingly) the white world into theirs while each day just a bit more of their blackness, and thus purpose, is stripped away. (See Thematic Issues section.)

Even those like Laurel who, unlike Winston Alcott, willingly accept the mores of this small society are forced to become tragic heroes when they cannot rise above its petty demands. Though Ruth Anderson's former friends like Laurel might pity her for her present circumstances with Norman, Ruth has been saved from the insanity of this maddening environment. Even Laurel once recalled that whenever she and Ruth conversed on the phone, she could detect pity in Ruth's voice for her instead of vice versa. Strangely enough Willa Nedeed, the erstwhile first lady of Linden Hills, longed to be like Laurel, while Laurel longed to possess Ruth's strength. Ironically, those who live in Linden Hills do not seem to have the stamina to survive Linden Hills.

The novel also presents minor characters whose purpose is to highlight the detrimental effect of living in Linden Hills. For example, Xavier Donnell and Maxwell Smyth are automobile industry executives who have lost, or are in the process of losing, a sense of themselves. Xavier sees Maxwell as the perfect mentor, given the fact that Maxwell has succeeded so well in the corporate world. However, Maxwell has done so at the expense of his cultural grounding. Not necessarily wanting to be white, Maxwell takes pride in being "no color at all" (106). Maxwell chides Xavier for dating Lester's sister Roxanne because, according to Maxwell, "that family has one foot in the ghetto and the other on a watermelon rind" (116). Maxwell has denied himself the privilege of marrying because he cannot find the proper woman to "accessorize" his accomplishments. A robot rather than a human being, Maxwell, whose dehumanization is intensified by living in Linden Hills, attempts to transform Xavier into a similarly emotionless vessel.

Some characters are beholden to the social codes and expectations of Linden Hills, while others seek to defy the system. Chester Parker subverts the Linden Hills social order when he hires Willie and Lester to assist in redecorating his deceased wife's room. Lycentia Parker has not even been buried when Chester asks the two to remove the wallpaper so that he can prepare to welcome his mistress into the house. Because Lycentia has been one of the most rigid of Linden Hills residents, Chester's desire to "cleanse" his house of any signs of her underscores his rejection of the propriety so tenaciously maintained in Linden Hills. A particular example of Chester's defiance is his insistence that Lester and Willie perform their work while Lycentia's wake is being held downstairs. Chester's rejection of Lycentia and all that she represented is also a reclamation of himself and his ideals. His actions offend the social code, but they are true to his own wishes.

Another character who defies the Linden Hills system is Rev. Michael Hollis. Ever since his wife left him eight years earlier as a result of his infidelity, Hollis has been confused and unfocused, a circumstance made worse by his alcoholism. Hollis also feels as though he has lost much of the passion he formerly brought to the ministry, partly as a result of his own failings but partly as a result of having become voluntarily constrained by the rigid and emotionless atmosphere of Linden Hills. In order to regain his passion, Hollis decides to preach a rousing sermon for Lycentia's funeral, regardless of what Luther Nedeed, funeral director and resident dictator, thinks. Fully aware that Linden Hills expects a sedate ceremony, Hollis decides instead to stun the community out of its passivity. And even though he is unsuccessful (the only person he stirs is Chester), and even though Luther takes control by restoring order upon delivering the eulogy, Hollis at least takes comfort in the act of defiance. Instead of blindly accepting the social dictates of Linden Hills, Hollis begins to govern himself.

While some characters embrace sterile Linden Hills and others try to resist its influence, those like Willie and Lester attempt a detached objectivity. Assisting them in this regard is Daniel Braithwaite, resident historian. Though he is a rather minor character, his significance is undeniable. On the one hand, Braithwaite seems like a weak character and an ineffectual human being. On the other, he emerges as a wise counselor. For several years, Braithwaite has compiled revealing data about the unique culture of Linden Hills, good and bad, yet he refuses to use the information in an effort to remedy some of the ills of the neighborhood. When Lester asks the historian why he will not "use [his] work to help save people" (262), Braithwaite responds that people will continue to live in Linden Hills no matter what he does. As an objective observer Braithwaite emphasizes the fact that ultimately human beings are responsible for their own lives. As a neutral party, he appreciates both the negative and the positive aspects of a Linden Hills residency.

THEMATIC ISSUES

Linden Hills examines the destructive effects on, and the fragmentation of, the black psyche when, at the expense of everything humane, African Americans focus entirely on re-creating a black version of the American dream. In this novel the dream becomes a nightmare. For several generations the Nedeed family has attempted to counteract the effects of institutional racism by constructing a neighborhood so well maintained and envied that even some whites want their adjacent communities associated with Linden Hills. Ever since the original Luther Nedeed purchased in 1820 the extensive parcel of land that would become Linden Hills, the Nedeed family has carefully and methodically chosen the various residents who would make up this planned community. And every generation of Nedeeds has stamped out any perceived threat to this vision: removing any black family who defies the dream; registering Linden Hills as a historical landmark to protect it from encroachment by the white neighborhood nearby; and in the case of every Luther Nedeed since 1837, seizing full control for raising the next heir (the next Luther) to the Nedeed fortune as well as, for the most part, severing emotional ties between mother and son.

Naylor addresses this theme of psychological fragmentation in its full complexity, never reducing it to simplistic or convenient explanations. On the one hand, it would seem that everything connected to the Nedeeds is evil and insidious and that the residents of Linden Hills are misguided pawns in one family's psychotic game of domination. On the other hand, the Nedeed dream is presented as an appropriate response to institutional white racism in its attempt to provide blacks with a sense of security, self-definition, and purpose. The paradox implied here is the focus of the text. If blacks succumb to racism, they are doomed; yet when they resist oppression they are fated for pain as well. Very subtly Naylor suggests that when fighting the evil of racism, by whatever means, one is destined to partake of a measure of that evil, especially when one loses focus on the purpose of the fight.

As the Linden Hills historian Dr. Daniel Braithwaite explains, the current generation of Linden Hills residents has lost "a sense of purpose about their history and their being" (260). The former generations understood the need to enforce a sense of black dignity and to defy the low expectations for black success; the simple act of attaining something previously beyond reach was sufficient in this effort, because the achievement was reward enough in creating a sense of pride. The neighborhood was to be made up of "black homes with black aspirations and histories—for good or evil" (261). For the former generations, moving into Linden Hills, establishing a cohesive black community, and then maintaining the sanctity of the community was that achievement. However, the latter generations lost sight of that dream in exchange for more and more material success, an obsession brought on in large measure, according to Braithwaite, by their having to go into the white world, or white corporate structure, to earn a living. Instead of selling their souls for Linden Hills as Lester seems to think, bits and bits of their souls (of their essence) have been taken away every time they enter that white world and attempt success on its terms, a success that is always just beyond their reach. In Braithwaite's estimation, then, dream turned nightmare is the result of transformed motivations on the part of residents. Instead of defining their residency in Linden Hills as a means of continued black cooperation, the inhabitants consider it simply "the thing to do." It is *the* place to be, but in the words of Braithwaite, "to be *what*?" (260). So fragmented now in their very beings, residents in Linden Hills have lost their humanity, a crucial and natural part of themselves.

This focus on the natural introduces yet another important theme: the natural versus the unnatural. There is much that is unnatural about Linden Hills. Family relationships are stilted and forced. Neighborliness is borne out of obligation, not altruism. And marital relationships are founded on assets, not love or passion. Anything that makes most residents human has been systematically "cultivated, or cultured" out of them. Serving textually as the best example of this dilemma is Maxwell Smyth, the personification of the unnatural. As the novel describes, "To even the most careful observer, this man seemed to have made the very *elements* disappear, while it was no more than the psychological sleight-of-hand that he used to make his *blackness* disappear" (my emphasis; 102). That Maxwell could seem to make the elements (natural entities) disappear would suggest his doing the impossible, the unnatural. And if he can make his blackness (the most natural trait he possesses) seem to disappear, he has indeed risen to the height of abnormality, or the unnatural. It is also important to note that Maxwell is presented as the epitome of Linden Hills success. But as Daniel Braithwaite has noted, this success in corporate America has cost Maxwell to strip himself of all that makes him a unique individual, including his blackness. The self-imposed stress under which Maxwell functions destroys Laurel Dumont, and given the meticulousness with which executives like these two must conduct their lives, it is no surprise. For example, Maxwell gave as much consideration to the decision when and if to smile as he did to the purchase of a new car. Conducting one's life with such precision would have to sap one of humanity bit by bit, especially one like Maxwell who has taken this battle with the natural to an extreme: he resists physical intimacy because he is uncomfortable with the heat and erratic motion of sex. In addition, he has regulated his food and liquid intake such that disposal of bodily solids is odor-free and inconsequential; in short, any act that would suggest he is human has been eliminated. The question that emerges, then, is "At what cost has Maxwell gained success in the white world?" Answer: he has lost his humanity.

This search for success, with the attendant results of fragmentation and the pursuit of the unnatural, also engenders domestic abuse of women, a theme addressed in *The Women of Brewster Place*. Here Naylor grapples with the notion that black women ultimately become sacrificial lambs when black men battle the demons of white racism outside the home; they receive the brunt of the anger that black men, for various reasons, cannot vent on white men and a larger racist society. In *Linden Hills*, even when the black man has achieved a level of success, sustaining that success renders him, in his own estimation, more vulnerable to the punishments of racism, and his concern becomes obsession that expresses itself negatively in a decided detachment from, or even anger toward (an internal anger projected on), the black woman. The bizarre nature of this emotional disturbance is made poignant in the Nedeed men's choice for wives. Every generation chooses a light-complexioned woman, yet each man wants her to produce a dark-skinned male like him. To be sure, the Nedeed men want to prove the potency of blackness over any complexion less than black, but at the same time, they are placing the women in the position for blame if this potency is not proven. The woman finds herself in an impossible situation, harkening back to slavery days. When Willa Prescott Nedeed produces a light-skinned son, her husband accuses her of adultery (and perhaps with a white man), but if she, like the other Nedeed brides, is of light hue, then a lighter strain is coursing through her veins and could easily reveal itself. That such has not occurred in previous generations is no guarantee that it cannot happen in the present day. But the present-day Luther will not consider that fact. So just like black women during slavery, Willa is doomed to criticism and/or abuse no matter her action. In the slave woman's case, if she tries to reject the sexual overtures of her white owner, she is beaten and/or raped; then if and when she produces a child as a result of the attack, she is victimized again by her black husband/companion when he deems her blameworthy. It is this history of black female victimization that Naylor addresses here, a history that always has at its core white male machinations or the machinations of the larger white patriarchal society.

HISTORICAL CONTEXT

Linden Hills focuses, to some degree, on the historical migratory practices of blacks from the antebellum days and beyond. Even before the Great Migration of the post–World War I period blacks looked to the North as a haven from the harsh realities of physical and emotional abuse they suffered in slavery. Instead of working unrewarded within the "peculiar institution" they sought a life wherein their efforts would benefit them and improve their way of life. Part of this migration before and after the Civil War would entail blacks' establishing their own towns, much like author Zora Neale Hurston's Eatonville, Florida; or other towns peppered throughout Oklahoma (later to be fictionalized in Toni Morrison's *Paradise*) and Kansas (particularly Nicodemus). In other towns blacks established businesses that thrived, ironically because blacks had no alternative but to support them since segregation often prevented them from patronizing white businesses. And in the case of Tulsa, Oklahoma, blacks built what was ultimately called the "Black Wall Street," because the black business district in that city boasted several successful businesses that served as a veritable national clearinghouse for networking with other black businesses throughout the country. Unfortunately, this thriving area was bombed in the 1920s because it offered too much competition with the white establishment. Even today, economic historians ponder what might have been, in the annals of black economic history, had the Oklahoma project lasted.

This novel traces, from 1820 to the early 1980s, the development of a carefully planned black community that would prove not only to white America but also to black America itself the potential of black people to succeed despite historical impediments. And though the community flourishes for several generations, it ultimately suffers once its inhabitants must leave the community in order to earn a living. In this way, the novel records the fate of typical black communities, ironically on the heels of the perceived success of integration. Once blacks could enter and then patronize previously all-white establishments, black businesses suffered. Likewise, when Linden Hills residents enter the white world to work, to trade, and subsequently to define themselves, they lose their original purpose for sustaining their own community: to maintain a comfortable way of life without immediate white intrusion and with the peace of mind and pride of having achieved the goal despite the former and continued opposition of racism. The ultimate horror is that the community of Linden Hills may perish as a result of such neglect.

In focusing on a successful middle- and upper middle-class black community, Naylor employs an important literary prototype that has come to define African-American literature: the concept of "inversion," initiated by slave narrator Olaudah Equiano (one of the few to chronicle a bondman's life in Africa before his enslavement). Rejecting the notion that black is equated automatically with savagery, evil, or bestiality, or that blacks/Africans are nothing more than objects, Vassa instead highlights in the first chapter of his autobiography a well-maintained, perfectly ordered African society wherein the inhabitants practice religion, fidelity to family, obedience to law, cleanliness, and modesty. The perception of African, or black, culture is "inverted." (See Literary Heritage chapter.)

LITERARY DEVICE AND GENRE

Naylor uses, and to some degree lampoons, this tradition of "inversion." In *Linden Hills* almost every physical or philosophical concept is reversed. To the outside world everything black (i.e., everything in Linden Hills) is to be envied, because these blacks have made themselves central to all external entities, including some whites who want to be associated with the community. Also, the route to social and economic prominence in Linden Hills is not upward, but downward; the most influential in the community, including Luther Nedeed, live at the bottom of the hill. And Luther, who ostensibly epitomizes civility and gentility, has, in an act of unprecedented barbarity, incarcerated his wife in a downstairs dungeon. With these examples, Naylor seems to suggest that merely supplanting white with black is not sufficient when neither the rules nor the game has truly changed; the paradigm of oppressed versus oppressor is still active.

Besides the African-American tradition of inversion Naylor also uses well-established European traditions. Traces of the Gothic novel (see Literary Heritage chapter) are evident in *Linden Hills*. From the mysterious and anachronistic Luther Nedeed (a mortician, he is consistently described as seeming to hail from another century), to the winding and rambling neighborhood (replacing in this case the usual sprawling mansion with its inexplicable occurrences and haunting noises), and culminating in the stock "crazy woman in the attic" character (in this novel, Willa Nedeed is locked away in the basement), *Linden Hills* succeeds as a modern Gothic work. And like her American predecessor Edgar Allan Poe, Naylor combines physical Gothic horror with psychological horror as she explores the impact of frustration, or thwarted desires, on the psyche. For example, Lester and Willie's friend Norman Anderson suffers from a strange disorder that results in hallucinations; he thinks that his skin is being consumed by a mysterious pink growth. No origin is given for the mental illness, nor is any remedy offered. The inexplicable ailment simply exists. Of course, Norman's malady symbolizes the various ailments plaguing residents throughout Linden Hills, and inasmuch as Norman's problem has no specific or immediate cause, neither do theirs.

Naylor also borrows from the picaresque tradition. (See Literary Heritage chapter.) In this novel, however, Naylor modifies the picaro, using two characters, Lester and Willie, to serve in this role. Each of the men embodies different aspects of a low-life character. Willie serves as a "geographical" rogue (he resides in poverty-stricken Putney Wayne and thus requires Lester's guidance throughout Linden Hills), while Lester serves as an "intellectual and emotional" rogue (though he is a resident of Linden Hills he has neither the intellectual nor the emotional maturity of Willie and thus requires Willie's guidance). Neither Willie nor Lester is gainfully employed; instead they are poets who spend much of their time honing their craft and reciting their creative wares in coffeehouses. Lester lives off the kindnesses begrudgingly of his mother and sister, while Willie periodically assumes menial jobs whenever he requires money. As they sojourn throughout Linden Hills, they encounter persons from different walks of life but who each have a stake in the maintenance of the community; their very lifelines are connected to the survival of this neighborhood. With Willie and Lester serving as careful observers, Naylor makes commentary on the foibles of an otherwise unsuspecting community.

To a lesser degree Naylor applies concepts from the epistolary novel (see Literary Heritage chapter), while also using the photograph and the ledger as narrative models. Each genre is used as a kind of substitute diary from the lives of the Nedeed women. In the Willa Nedeed sections of the novel, Willa plods through the writings of the Nedeed wives and mothers who preceded her. Luwana Packerville Nedeed wrote letters to herself as she tried to retain her sanity once she realized that she had no power in the Nedeed house. Evelyn Creton Nedeed recorded every food purchase needed for the many recipes she perfected in order to add structure to her otherwise empty life. Priscilla McGuire Nedeed kept a photograph album to record, and extract some meaning from, her life with the Nedeeds. With each of these characters, Naylor explores how history is recorded (what methods are used), who is recording it (and why), and most importantly, who is interpreting it (and with what agenda). Clearly, the person who has the opportunity to leave a written record enjoys a level of power unavailable to someone who is denied the chance.

It is obvious that Naylor challenges the reader with these concepts, especially given the descriptions of Lester and Willie, the main characters. While both are poets, Lester writes his creations, but Willie only commits his to memory. His devotion to the oral tradition seems to be key to his retaining a sense of himself. Though to write is to assume some power, to write is also to relinquish power when one exposes the creative product for the interpretation of others. So while Naylor acknowledges the significance of the written word, she also pays homage to the primacy of the spoken word.

NARRATIVE TECHNIQUE

While the narrative is propelled by the daily encounters of Willie Mason and Lester Tilson, neither of these main characters narrates. Instead, Naylor relies, in her typical fashion, on the omniscient third-person narrator (an omniscient narrator has insight into the thoughts and feelings of characters). This perspective allows the reader to penetrate the thoughts of the many characters who people the novel. Naylor opens the novel with an extended prologue that foregrounds the history not only of Linden Hills but also, at least tangentially, of America. In its totality the novel encompasses over 150 years, from roughly 1820 to the very early 1980s. The novel is then divided into six chapters, the headings of which are the six days of December just prior to Christmas, from December 19 (the first chapter) to December 24 (the last chapter). On each day self-fashioned handymen Willie and Lester set out to earn money while also observing the behaviors, critiquing the mores, and exposing the foibles of an otherwise unsuspecting Linden Hills. Unlike *The Women of Brewster Place*, in which Naylor focused on a particular character per chapter, the *Linden Hills* chapters detail the stories of a host of characters. This technique serves the work well, especially since Naylor also crafts a well-developed subplot, the details of which must also be peppered throughout the main narrative.

In her inimitable style, Naylor ignores both linear structure and prescribed boundaries. Even though the reader can trace Lester and Willie's movements chronologically, as indicated in the chapter headings, Naylor disrupts this structure by interposing throughout the main narrative the subplot details of the Willa Nedeed story. And within the Willa story, Naylor uses the flashback to present the lives of ancestral Nedeed women. In short, the Willa history disrupts the linear movement of the Willie and Lester escapade. In terms of resisting prescribed boundaries (that is, developing only one genre), Naylor relies not just on one narrative mode, but on several. In addition to the straight-line narrative of the third person, Naylor uses, if only briefly, the epistolary format, poetry, biblical reference, diary, and stream of consciousness (a point of view that seeks to capture the unorganized, random flow of the mind). In this way, Naylor uses narrative structure to underscore one of the issues that recurs not only in *Linden Hills* but also in her subsequent works: the necessity of questioning and then rejecting the imposition of arbitrary boundaries. In an eloquent exchange early in Linden Hills, Willie and Lester discuss the idiocy of enclosing, for example, a university campus with a fence, while the gate remains open. Lester points out that its only function is "To get you used to the idea that what they have in there is different, special"(45). Lester then questions why an individual, one for example who wants to be a doctor, cannot simply enter a library, read all he can, and then sit for an qualifying exam. But because society needs a system of "them and us" (a way of segregating humanity), it must establish boundaries that ultimately have nothing to do with reality. Lester's questioning this need merely reinforces the broader question that Naylor is raising not only in narrative content, but also in narrative structure.

AN INTERTEXTUAL ANALYSIS

An intertextual critique assesses the similarity between two works of literature. Generally the text being analyzed is compared to a more established, or classical, text. Often the writer of the second work is either paying homage to the established writer or parodying some aspect of the writer's work. The task of the critic is to highlight the extent to which such modeling supports the aesthetic, philosophical, or thematic quality of the work being analyzed; and to what extent the association succeeds. For example, if a twentieth-century novelist borrows creatively from Shakespeare, does the novelist appropriate Shakespeare's material merely for aesthetic purposes, or is the writer drawing a comparison between the time setting of the Shakespearean play and the setting of the novel? Or is the writer merely comparing character types, a novel's protagonist with a Shakespearean hero? The intertextual analysis encourages the critic to become even more familiar with the established text and to further appreciate the primacy of that work.

Naylor loosely bases *Linden Hills* on Part I of Dante's epic poem *The Divine Comedy* (1321), entitled "The Inferno." In this section of the work the Italian poet Dante is guided through hell by Vergil, the great classical poet whom Dante considers the embodiment of the highest knowledge attainable by the human mind. After passing through the anteroom, housed by those who did nothing in life good or bad, the two travelers begin to descend throughout the nine levels of hell, encountering along the way such derelicts as unbaptized spirits (first level), carnal sinners (second level), gluttons (third level), misers (fourth level), the wrathful (fifth level), heretics (sixth level), the violent (seventh level), the fraudulent (eighth level), traitors (an ice-locked ninth level), and then ultimately Lucifer, who is manifested in a three-headed figure. Upon entering the sixth level (and thereafter), the poets witness the horrible, and generally fiery, torments of the City of Dis.

To accommodate this Dantean structure, Naylor, in addition to presenting two poets, constructs Linden Hills as a nine-tiered neighborhood, with street names extending from First Crescent Drive (at the top of Linden Hills) to Fifth Crescent Drive. Then, due to a long-ago conflict in the neighborhood, Tupelo Drive begins at what would have been Sixth Crescent and extends through the next four tiers. Once entering what would have been Sixth Crescent Drive, then, one is entering the most horrific levels in the neighborhood (as in the sixth level of hell noted above). Each of Naylor's major story lines occurs on one of the nine Linden Hills tiers. The Laurel Dumont suicide story (on what would have been Sixth Crescent Drive) introduces the reader to Tupelo Drive, the street that ends at Luther Nedeed's estate. The most affluent area of Linden Hills is, of course, at the bottom; and it is therefore the most spiritually bankrupt dimension. At the very bottom of the hill is Luther Nedeed, the Lucifer-like character, whose ultimate betrayal of his wife and son will lead to the fiery climax at the end. Re-creating Dante's three-headed figure, Naylor collapses Luther, Willa, and Sinclair into one massive burning bulk that must be carted out whole in the final scene of the novel.

Just as Dante and Vergil survive at the end of "The Inferno" by escaping through a tunnel surrounded by water left to journey through "Purgatory" (Part II) and ultimately "Paradise" (Part III), Willie and Lester escape over the moat around the Nedeed estate and land in the adjacent snow-laden cemetery. And like Dante, each of these young poets is left to ponder the lessons of the journey, perhaps to gain insight into human foibles or undergo a significant revelation, as does Dante.

Yet another intertextual reading is applicable between *Linden Hills* and Edgar Allan Poe's Gothic tale "The Fall of the House of Usher." This story chronicles the events attendant to the visit of an unnamed narrator to the mansion of his boyhood friend, Roderick Usher. Upon his arrival the narrator begins both to recall, and to notice in the present moment, strange attributes of his friend and the family. For instance, the entire Usher family line, for several generations, has maintained only a direct line of descent. And Roderick Usher seems to suffer from an inexplicable malady whereby all of his senses are heightened to such an extent that he can withstand only the dullest stimuli. In addition, his twin sister Madeleine is catatonic, and when in the course of the story she dies, the narrator and Roderick bury her in the cellar below. At the end of the story Madeleine returns from the dead and collapses on her brother, at which time the narrator flees from the house just seconds before it implodes, in an inferno-like occurrence, into an adjacent tarn.

The final scene of *Linden Hills* clearly bows to this story. Willa, much like Madeleine, is practically buried alive in the basement, prevented by Luther from returning upstairs until she forces her way, with the help of Willie, to the main level of the house. Like the Ushers, the Nedeeds, in a psychotic need for both biological and ultimately social control, allow only a direct line of descent. And like the Ushers, the Nedeeds perish in their own towering inferno, while Poe's narrator, like Willie and Lester (and Vergil and Dante), escapes via water (the moat surrounding the Usher house). Clearly, many of the Gothic elements in *Linden Hills* are grounded in the Poe tradition.

5

Mama Day
(1988)

With *Mama Day* Naylor charts a different literary terrain. While her first two novels were grounded in known reality, this third novel allows Naylor to explore, and to question, the concept of reality. Set on a mystical island off the southeast coast, *Mama Day* forces the reader to suspend disbelief and to shed those faculties normally used to navigate the established world. *Mama Day* is at once a romantic tale chronicling the emergent relationship of main characters Cocoa and George and also a narrative enigma that delineates every possible influence on this relationship: familial, historical, psychological, social, gendered, spiritual, and mystical. With this broad analysis, Naylor encourages the reader to consider the various factors that shape our lives.

PLOT DEVELOPMENT

In *Mama Day* Gloria Naylor questions the notion of fixed reality and offers instead an analysis of individual definitions of, and responses to, reality. The novel focuses on the budding relationship, and later marriage, of Ophelia (Cocoa) Day and George Andrews, residents of New York City. Because they hail from different backgrounds, Cocoa and George enjoy divergent sensibilities and philosophies. Cocoa is a southerner from a small island off the coast of (but not a part of either) South

Carolina and Georgia. Presented as a magical and mystical place, Willow
Springs is a world unto itself, with no legal or cultural ties to the mainland. George is a native New Yorker, and unlike Cocoa who was raised
by family (her grandmother and great-aunt), George was raised in an
orphanage. And though his early life was not as harsh as it might have
been, he was raised with little opportunity for frivolous activity. His was
a practical upbringing, and everything he does subsequent to leaving the
orphanage has been planned, focused, and determined. Cocoa, on the
other hand, has been catered to by her grandmother Abigail and even
by her great-aunt Miranda (Mama Day), though Mama Day has also
enforced discipline.

Cocoa meets George in August 1980 when she goes to his engineering
firm, where he is co-partner, seeking employment as a receptionist. She
is not awarded the job, but George, unbeknown to Cocoa, helps to secure
Cocoa a job with one of the firm's clients. In this way, George and Cocoa
retain periodic contact, though each denies a romantic interest in the
other, Cocoa thinking George too reserved and aloof and George thinking Cocoa too exacting. Nevertheless, soon after Cocoa assumes her new
job, George invites her to dinner. The interaction is strained at best, un-
salvageable at worst. However, George still wants to see Cocoa, mainly
because he wants to convince her that even after seven years, she has
not come to appreciate the real New York. In short, he wants to introduce
her to his world, not as an outsider or a tourist, but as a participant. For
several weekends following, George serves as Cocoa's host as he strives
to transform her opinion of the city and its people. Before she met
George, Cocoa identified persons of different ethnic groups by the
food(s) associated with that group, a mode of reference offensive to
George. Within a few weeks of their "courtship," Cocoa engages less in
stereotype and comes to appreciate the wealth of New York's diversity.
Suspending her former belief system in favor of George's perspective of
the city, Cocoa uncovers and discovers an entirely new home for herself,
and just as she embarks on a new relationship with George. By January
1981 Cocoa and George are married.

The early phase of their marriage is fraught with the typical adjust-
ments: sharing space, dividing domestic responsibilities, managing
household finances, all the while trying to retain individual identities.
And for the first four years, George still insisted on their taking separate
vacations, he to the Super Bowls every January and she back to Willow
Springs for her annual August homecoming. Cocoa would have pre-
ferred to travel with George, but she tries to remain sensitive to his

passion for sports, which she does not share, and to his obsession with work projects (major ones that always surfaced in August). Finally, in 1985 George agrees to accompany Cocoa to Willow Springs, a decision that would render their lives changed forever.

Even though George does not meet Abigail and Mama Day for four years, he has spoken with them numerous times on the phone, and he has favored them with gifts and money in the interim. In this fashion he has ingratiated himself with the older women, who have since the marriage admonished Cocoa not to badger George about his busy schedule. Satisfied that George is a decent and sincere man, who loves Cocoa unconditionally, they have been content to meet him in his own time. Needless to say, when the day finally arrives, all of Willow Springs is abuzz with excitement, though Mama Day tries to mask her enthusiasm. Never to be outdone or outwitted, she maintains a calm demeanor while Abigail is practically manic as the time approaches.

George and Cocoa's visit to Willow Springs comprises the second half of this two-part novel. Consequently, the inhabitants of Willow Springs assume a prominent role in the work, especially title character Mama Day. Now ninety years old, Mama Day serves the island as a healer, mentor, counselor, and spiritualist. And though no one would openly refer to her as a conjure woman, her leanings toward the occult are suspect. Both Mama Day and her sister Abigail embody the somewhat surreal quality of Willow Springs. When George first meets the two women, he comments on their rather youthful demeanor, as their spirits seem to defy their eighty-five-and ninety-year-old bodies. It becomes immediately apparent that Willow Springs is another world that is guided by its own rules, mores, and sensibilities. The reality that has defined George's New York existence will do little good in this marginal place.

Soon after their arrival on the island, George and Cocoa undergo noticeable transformations. While George begins to relish his stay on the island, Cocoa becomes more agitated. To some degree, she is a bit jealous of the way not only her family but also the other residents have taken to George. Ever since she left Willow Springs, Cocoa has always managed to separate her Willow Springs life from her city life. This compartmentalization of her life has given her balance so that no matter what was occurring in her work and personal life, she could always depend on Willow Springs to be her childhood sanctuary. Leaving it as a separate place retained its innocence, and hence her own. But now that she has come home with her husband, Cocoa is forced to reconcile these two worlds. And even though she complained during the first four years of her marriage that George would not accompany her to Willow Springs, she now finds his presence on the island unsettling. Ironically, George seems, at least initially, to have acclimated himself quite well to the place and the people of Willow Springs. Because Cocoa is accustomed to enjoying undivided attention when she returns home, she is mildly frustrated that she must now share the spotlight with her husband. On the one hand, she is pleased that family and friends like George, but on the other hand, she is offended that her marriage somehow validates her in a way that she never before experienced.

In having to reconcile (in essence, marry) her two worlds, Cocoa is forced to mature and accept new challenges. In many ways, her entire relationship with George has been a vehicle for growth. This visit to Willow Springs provides yet another phase of this development. Because George never had a real family, he seems to thrive in the hospitality of the Day family. And once the matriarchs Abigail and Mama Day realize George's gratitude, they love him even more. Soon he is tirelessly performing chores at the homes of both women, further ingratiating himself with them and stunning Cocoa with his charm.

Soon, however, matters take a turn for the worse. One of the island's inhabitants, Ruby, an ostensible friend of the Days but one who is now suspicious and jealous of Cocoa, places a curse on Cocoa, the result of which is Cocoa's systematic physical and emotional deterioration. While George can see that Cocoa's condition is worsening, he is ill-equipped to comprehend the nature of her sickness. Appreciating the skepticism of a very practical-minded engineer and not wanting to shatter his reality by schooling him on Willow Springs reality, both Abigail and Mama Day are reluctant to tell him the truth (the Willow Springs truth). It becomes apparent, though, that George will have to learn of the "otherworld" practices of Willow Springs if he is to see his wife healthy once again.

Cocoa's sickness occurs during one of the worst hurricanes that Willow Springs has experienced in the present century. As a consequence, the one bridge that leads to the mainland (the outside world) is destroyed, as are all phone and radio connections. Willow Springs, then, is completely isolated from the world that George knows. As none of the science, practicality, or reason that he relies on can help him or Cocoa, George thinks he has entered a nightmare from which he will never awake.

It is at this stage that the imaginary—from both the reader's and George's perspective—world of Willow Springs takes precedence in the novel. As a means of trying to help in the recovery of her great-niece,

Mama Day retires to the ancestral home of the Days, referred to as "the other place" and located in a remote section of the island beyond the family cemetery. The family home is a mystical place where known reality is less discernible. In addition to coming here periodically to gather medicinal herbs, Mama Day often seeks sanctuary in the other place to commune with her ancestors and to seek guidance as she tackles yet another modern dilemma. There is none more baffling than Cocoa's ailment.

After the hurricane subsides, Cocoa's condition worsens. Suffering not only from lethargy but also from hallucinations, Cocoa almost submits to her "curse." However, Mama Day knows that she can be saved, but only with the help of George. Somehow she must convince him of the "truth" of Ruby's curse on Cocoa, because only if he believes, or at least suspends his disbelief, will he be of any substantial help. Desperate for his wife's recovery and denied access to the world he knows and understands, George, though reluctantly, acquiesces to Mama Day's demand that he, first, visit her at the other place and, second, participate in a rather provincial ritual. Instructed to retrieve the contents of a particular hen's nest from Mama Day's chicken coop and return to the other place, George is supposed to prove his willingness to connect with Willow Springs reality, which is, of course, an integral part of Cocoa's heritage. According to Mama Day, if Cocoa is to be healed, every one of her closest human connections, especially George to whom she is bonded legally, spiritually, and emotionally, must embrace Willow Springs truths.

In his pursuit, however, George, who is plagued with a weak heart, is attacked by the chickens, suffers heart failure, and dies. He still succeeds in saving Cocoa, though, because he gives his life in sacrifice for hers. Soon after George's death, Cocoa begins to recover and ultimately regains her former vitality. Three years after his death, Cocoa remarries and, in the ensuing years, gives birth to two sons, naming one after George in honor of her undying love for him and in respect for the sacrifice he made for her.

CHARACTER DEVELOPMENT

Major characters in this novel include Cocoa Day Andrews, George Andrews, Miranda (Mama) Day, Abigail Day, and Ruby. Because the novel, for the most part, charts Cocoa and George's emergent relationship, from courtship through marriage to George's death, and because George and Cocoa serve as the predominant narrators, the focus is primarily on them. In the course of this work, each of them grows as an individual and as a partner. As they hail from two different worlds (two different cultures), each serves as the perfect sparring partner for the other. Early on they learn that differences breed exposure to the unknown, and in demystifying the unknown, they develop into more emotionally substantive beings.

An orphan who is raised in a state shelter for boys, George, given only the basics of life, is taught early on not to expect much from the future. Instead, Mrs. Jackson, the shelter's stern but fair matron, teaches, "Only the present has potential, sir" (26). As a result, before he meets Cocoa, George has lived according to this one precept, taking one day at a time and relying only on himself. George is practical and independent to a fault. Never a dreamer, he has simply worked diligently every day of his life, making his way through college and ultimately establishing himself as a partner in the Andrews & Stein Engineering Firm. Though his way has rendered him successful in his professional life, his personal life has gone unfulfilled, that is, until he meets Cocoa.

Once she enters his life George is challenged to become less rigid and more flexible. Even the single act of meeting Cocoa begins to transform George's world from one of normal absolutes to one of mystery, imagination, and the unknown. George and Cocoa officially meet when she enters his firm to inquire about an advertised job, but they encounter each other earlier in the day at a coffee shop not too far from the firm. Recounting in the narrative the feelings he experiences upon seeing Cocoa bent over her newspaper and coffee, George states, "The feeling is so strong, it almost physically stops me: *I will see that neck again. . . .* That is the feeling I actually had, while the feeling I quickly exchanged it with was: *I've seen this woman before. . . . And just imagine, Miss Day, when I passed you I said to myself, Wouldn't it be funny if I saw her again?*" (27–28). Right away Cocoa forces George out of his "only the present has potential" mode. In considering these various "meetings" with Cocoa, George is dismantling the fixed boundaries between past, present, and future. For the first time in his life George is considering the possibility of spiritual connections, mystical alliances, that defy explanations and logical conclusions.

However, duly shaken by such novel realizations, George concludes that any future interactions with Cocoa would be unwise and decides, therefore, to deny her the job. Nevertheless, George will ultimately come to appreciate this woman who disrupts his equilibrium and, in turn, he will develop into a selfless man who ingratiates himself easily with Cocoa's family.

Cocoa also changes as a result of her marriage to George. Because she is an only child, and because she was raised by her grandmother, Miss Abigail, who feels a particular obligation to make this parentless child happy, Cocoa is somewhat spoiled and self-centered, though not in an irredeemable way. Also instrumental in her life has been Mama Day, who has tempered Abigail's leniency with discipline and structure. Consequently, Cocoa has developed into an independent woman, exemplified in the fact that she has left her southern home and has made a life for herself in New York. Still, when she and George begin dating, she deliberately tests him for no reason other than to play childish games. She insists that he prove over and over again his love for her. George is passionate about sports, especially professional football. During the season, his only request is that Monday nights be honored as his television night. However, Cocoa complains that if he loves her, he would be willing to forgo those nights every so often. But when George presses her on the issue and asks if she has some specific request for a Monday night out, Cocoa demurs. George then gets angry and accuses Cocoa of being insensitive, stating that she evidently wants to torture him for the mere sake of torture, because if she truly has no specific need on a Monday night, why must they engage in a needless hypothetical discussion.

At one point during the courtship George considers purchasing a VCR so that he can record the Monday-night games but then decides not to, thinking instead that if he and Cocoa are to have a future, she will have to accept some aspects of his life. Ultimately, Cocoa will compromise, and for the first four years of their marriage, she accepts the fact that she and George will take separate vacations, when he insists on attending the annual Super Bowl games. That George provides an opportunity for Cocoa to grow and to compromise is evident in comments Mama Day makes upon learning, via Cocoa's periodic letters, of the conflicts in the courtship: "She's hard-headed and she's spoiled, and this is one who won't let her have her way. I'm starting to like him already" (109). Mama Day is certain that there must be something special about this new boyfriend, because George is the first man whom Cocoa has introduced to her family, even via letter. And Mama Day, pleased that Cocoa has met a man who will not relent to her every desire, appreciates the fact that Cocoa's continued development as a person and as a woman is contingent on her being challenged and defied at every opportunity.

In short, Cocoa's and George's growth is dependent on their remaining bonded to each other. That is why it is significant that they narrate the bulk of the novel. Each is writing to the other in an effort to record all of those feelings, anxieties, frustrations, and joys that punctuated their life together. Even after George's death (he, after all, is writing from the grave) and even after Cocoa's new marriage, Cocoa and George are still connected. He relinquishes his life for hers; and she, in compensation for that sacrifice, honors him not only by naming her second son George but also by documenting his life and by acknowledging his continued impact on her, even fourteen years after his death.

As title character and as matriarch of the Days, Mama Day serves as foundational character for the entire novel. Even before the focus moves completely to Willow Springs in the second half, Mama Day's presence is felt consistently in the New York segments, not only because Cocoa's visits to Willow Springs are interspersed in these segments, but also because Mama Day observes, assesses, and even impacts Cocoa's life from afar. She is an integral part of all that affects Cocoa. When Cocoa makes her first trip home after interviewing for the job at George's firm, she tells Mama Day and her grandmother Abigail that she will not get the job because the bosses wanted her to start work right away, and since she simply would not forgo her annual trip to Willow Springs, she knows they will not hold the job for her. Nevertheless, Mama Day urges Cocoa to write to the firm, thank them for their consideration, and inform them that she is still interested in employment. Though Cocoa thinks this will do no good, she, at least in her estimation, humors Mama Day and writes.

Completing the task, Cocoa gives the letter to Mama Day who insists on mailing it herself. Upon receiving the letter George admits that he had almost forgotten about Cocoa, and when he opens the envelope he notices a fine powder has been sprinkled inside. Unable to identify what it is, George finds himself reluctant to brush it away. From all indications the letter (the writing of which Mama Day initiated) has potentially served a dual purpose: sparking George's memory of Cocoa and renewing his affection for her. It is obvious that Mama Day sprinkled the mysterious powder in the envelope. Unbeknown to Cocoa, then, Mama Day, with her mystical prowess, is partially responsible for Cocoa's relationship and ultimate marriage. From the very beginning of the novel Mama Day is presented as a forceful woman who perhaps possesses supernatural powers.

All of the inhabitants of Willow Springs respect Mama Day's skills, whether in healing the sick or in warding off what they think may be curses exacted on them by an ominous practitioner. Even Dr. Smithfield, the mainland physician who visits the island in extreme cases, bows to Mama Day's ability. That Dr. Smithfield admires Mama Day adds credibility to her practice, even though she needs no such validation. Because she believes in the primacy of, and has witnessed the success of, natural cures, Mama Day feels obliged to offer her services whenever they are requested. And since she takes her job seriously, she absolutely refuses to be compared to the likes of Dr. Buzzard, the island's resident bootlegger, conjure man, con artist, and gambling cheat. Soon after George arrives with Cocoa in Willow Springs, he meets up with Buzzard, who proudly informs him that Mama Day is a bit jealous of the competition he offers to her practice, that they have a little professional rivalry afoot. When Mama Day hears of this insult she is incensed that the "shiftless, no-good, slew-footed, twisted-mouthed, slimy-backed" (191) Buzzard would even speak her name.

Clearly, Mama Day thinks that Buzzard somehow diminishes her efforts in doing legitimate work. Any practice that smacks of voodoo Mama Day disdains, and she would never identify herself as such. Still, when Cocoa suffers her debilitating illness at the hands of Ruby, the extremely jealous practitioner of the occult and victim of low self-esteem, Mama Day realizes that she must battle this adversity in kind. Calling upon all the fortitude she can muster from the other place, Mama Day connects the rational world with the mystical world when she asks George to honor the promise he made to Cocoa in the rational world, but to do so by obeying the rules of Willow Springs. In a phone conversation with Mama Day soon after he and Cocoa marry, George assures her, "She [Cocoa] has all I have" (136). Later challenging him, Mama Day wants George to open up his life just enough to accept an important part of Cocoa's Willow Springs world. Of course, in order to do so, he must suspend his rational beliefs from the outside world. Though the ritual that Mama Day insists he perform may seem ludicrous and ill-fated, he must execute the task. As the voice of reason and promise (which entails hope and having faith in the unknown), Mama Day, in fact, must bridge these two worlds. As a vital figure in the novel, she remains consistent throughout, believing in the possibilities of a better day even when circumstances seem to indicate otherwise.

While Mama Day has been responsible for providing Cocoa with discipline, Abigail has been the source of comfort and encouragement, most often coddling and spoiling her granddaughter. In short, Abigail functions as a foil to Mama Day. Early in the novel when Mama Day and Abigail are drafting one of their responses to Cocoa's monthly letters, it is Abigail's responsibility to write and to temper whatever harsh comments Mama Day has made. With painstaking effort Abigail forms euphemisms to mitigate what she considers Mama Day's offensive tone. And during some of Cocoa's visits, when Cocoa gets angry at Mama Day for trying to run her life yet again (Mama Day especially disdains Cocoa's insistence on accompanying her old friends to social clubs) and threatens to shorten her visit and leave, it is Abigail who must intervene, salve egos, and convince Cocoa to stay. Because she is the tamer of the two women, one might perceive her to be a flat character, but she ultimately emerges as strong and as determined as Mama Day or Cocoa.

Appearing only sparingly in the first half of the novel, Abigail emerges more fully in the second half, once George and Cocoa arrive in Willow Springs. Her strength of character is revealed during Cocoa's illness. Even as Cocoa's condition worsens, Abigail remains steadfast in her determination to be strong. Never attempting to force George to participate in Mama Day's ritual, never badgering him about his obligations as a husband and soul mate, Abigail simply shows her own concern by caring for Cocoa in a quiet, unobtrusive, selfless manner. And though Cocoa is mostly incoherent during the height of her ailment, even she appreciates Abigail's fortitude and sincerity "Reflected off the clear brown of her irises" (287). The trustworthiness of Abigail's eyes highlights the loyalty of the woman, and her refusal to shed tears underscores her determination to be a stabilizing force during this tragedy. Resisting melodramatic outbursts, Abigail instead validates the seriousness of Cocoa's illness by not redirecting the focus on herself. By the time the novel ends, Abigail has been dead for nine years, having died five years after George. She lived to fulfill her promise, to see Cocoa returned to health. But after she is confident that Cocoa has made not only a physical recovery, but also a reasonable emotional recovery, Abigail finally takes her sleep, as her duty has been fulfilled.

Ruby emerges as the villain by the end of the novel. Because she is jealous of Cocoa's happy marriage (her own marriage to a younger Junior Lee is in shambles) and because she feels threatened by Cocoa, Ruby decides to put a "curse" on Cocoa. Even though Cocoa survives the illness caused by the curse, because George's life is sacrificed to save Cocoa, Ruby has indirectly caused George's death. Throughout the greater portion of the novel, Ruby seems like a minor character, yet she is a major plot tool. Her presence changes the lives of George and Cocoa forever.

Minor characters include Bernice and Ambush Duvall, Pearl Duvall, and Dr. Buzzard. Bernice and Ambush, childhood friends of Cocoa, serve as the model married couple, each devoted to the other unconditionally despite the negative attitude of Ambush's mother Pearl. The Duvalls have been trying for some time to conceive a child, and because Pearl latches on to any excuse to criticize Bernice, she spares no opportunity to blame Bernice for the infertility. Bernice and Ambush emerge as likable characters, in part for their kind natures and in part because of their stark difference from Pearl, whose self-righteous behavior makes her less attractive to all. Sympathetic to Ambush and Bernice, Mama Day, at Bernice's urging, agrees to "assist" them in conceiving. Mama Day, unlike the self-absorbed Pearl, humors Bernice by supplying her with different herbs and by providing her with tasks to occupy her time, because she understands that Bernice has become high strung in her impatience to be pregnant. Dr. Buzzard serves as Mama Day's nemesis because of his unabashed experimentation with the occult. Though everyone on the island knows that Mama Day practices magic, she does not openly admit her leanings. And to have anyone believe that she and Buzzard are "colleagues" is offensive to Mama Day.

THEMATIC ISSUES

The bridge connecting Willow Springs to the U.S. mainland serves as an important symbol. One of the key thematic issues in the novel is "bridging," or drawing comparisons between seemingly disparate entities. The title character, Mama Day, serves an important role in this function. A bridge between the rational world and the mystical world, Mama Day underscores the necessity of being receptive to various forms of reality. Anytime she requires inspiration, Mama Day retires to the other place where she can commune with the spirits of her ancestors, and after receiving their messages, she returns to her regular life to be guided by what she has learned. By portraying Mama Day as the stabilizing force in the novel, Naylor validates both Mama Day's mystical presence and her rational presence. In this way, neither world takes precedence over the other. One's imaginative reality becomes as important, as one's sensate reality, and sometimes more so.

On yet another level Willow Springs represents the imaginative world, while the U.S. mainland (more precisely, New York) represents the sensate world. During the early stages of the novel, much comment is made about the difference between Cocoa's Willow Springs existence and her New York identity, a contrast brought on largely by her belief that the two locales are markedly different. Reconciling the differences between these two settings introduces yet another important theme: self-discovery. Part of Cocoa's discovery, and self-discovery, in fostering a relationship with George is uncovering the similarities between the two places. Highlighting these similarities while trying to school Cocoa on the uniqueness of New York, George describes the city as "a network of small towns . . . a handful of blocks, a single square mile hidden off with its own language, newspapers, and magazines—its own laws and codes of behavior, and sometimes even its own judge and juries" (61). New York, then, is composed of individual enclaves that project their own identity, much like Willow Springs. When Mama Day accompanies Cocoa to New York after George's death, she discovers these similarities. Instead of accepting Cocoa's suggestion that she take a guided tour of the city, Mama Day wanders about alone, visiting tourist traps and also meeting some of the people of New York. That Mama Day would find "right nice folks" in the city suggests again an apparent link between it and Willow Springs.

As the relationship between George and Cocoa dominates the novel, it is important to note how the theme of "bridging" functions with their story. Early on George and Cocoa are described as being very different, in terms of personality, family background, personal expectations, and general temperament. Cocoa complains that George is too exacting in his ways and not very imaginative, while George argues that simply sharing space with a woman is challenge enough. Yet as different as they are, an inexplicable quality draws them to each other. Their emerging relationship—confusing, mysterious, erratic, yet enduring and magnetic—defines the paradoxical nature of life that Naylor is highlighting. That we accept the mysterious nature of relationships (no two people who are radically different can explain why each is drawn to the other) but perhaps cannot accept the validity of other mysteries is, to be sure, contradictory and confusing. But in linking the George/Cocoa marriage to various opposing entities, Naylor forces the reader to examine the discrepancy. This point is made abundantly clear when Mama Day, in her attempt to convince George that he must engage in the mystical ritual in order to save Cocoa's life, reminds George that he and Cocoa are linked together in an intangible, yet binding way. And because of this emotional bond, one that defies simple logic, George must function in the Willow Springs world if he is to save his wife: "You see, she done bound more than her flesh up with you. And since she's suffering from something more than the flesh, I can't do a thing without you" (294). In addition to highlighting the mystical bond between George and Cocoa, Mama Day also highlights the link between the mysticism of that bond and the mysticism (inexplicable circumstances) of Cocoa's illness, which entails the mysticism of the Willow Springs world.

While focusing on the relationship of George and Cocoa it is also important to note the narrative structure of the novel and its impact on the bridging theme. As noted earlier, both George and Cocoa, with little interruption, share narrative duties, as they speak intermittently to each other about their life together. George is, of course, narrating from the grave, and as such, he links death with life. Just as Mama Day bridges the gap between life and death when she visits the other place to commune with the spirit of her ancestors, George's narrative sections make a similar bridge. Though he is dead, he still impacts Cocoa's present life, and the memory of their life together will always be a part of Cocoa's existence.

Still another significant link made in the novel is the one between the past and the present. Of course, Mama Day constructs such a link when she visits the ancestral home located at the other place; even stronger links between past and present are made in the plight of Bernice Duvall and in the plight of Mama Day's and Abigail's mother Ophelia (for whom Cocoa was named). Bernice comes to Mama Day to request Mama Day's assistance in helping her get pregnant. Having tried to give her husband a child for some time now, Bernice is desperate to ensure Duvall offspring. Ultimately, Bernice conceives and later gives birth to little Charles, whose short life spans the length of George and Cocoa's marriage, 1981–1985. How he dies is a mystery never solved, but his death is especially tragic to a mother like Bernice who wanted nothing more than to give her husband a child. Her loss is linked to the loss suffered by Ophelia Day in 1900. When Mama Day (Miranda) was five and Abigail was three, Ophelia mistakenly dropped their baby sister Peace down a well, a tragedy from which Ophelia never recovered and one that has forever plagued the family. When Peace (now a mystical and allegorical figure) was lost, peace was lost.

Ophelia's loss is linked not only to Bernice, but also to Cocoa. Though Abigail regrets the day her own daughter Grace named her baby Ophelia

(Cocoa) and, in so doing, visits upon Cocoa the horrors of Ophelia's tortured life, somehow Mama Day and Abigail are comforted that Cocoa, by being the child of Grace (allegorically, grace), will survive whatever ills befall her. These details reveal varying connections. Ophelia's tragedy is linked to Cocoa by virtue of ancestry and by virtue of Cocoa's given name (Ophelia). Bernice's loss, as a mother, is linked to Ophelia's and is thus indirectly linked to Cocoa's. But Bernice's loss is also directly linked to Cocoa's ultimate tragedy (the loss of George), because little Charles lived the exact number of years that Cocoa and George's marriage lasted. The act of saving Cocoa and sacrificing George becomes part of a larger story of healing and recovery, two concepts that emerge as secondary themes. In rescuing Cocoa, peace (recall Peace) is restored, and Ophelia's pain is put to rest.

HISTORICAL CONTEXT

In placing this story on a practically uncharted, and all-black, island, one officially unconnected to any mainland state, Naylor bows to an almost forgotten component of African-American history. Just as Africans were imported to various coastal regions on the eastern seaboard in the antebellum days, many were also imported to islands off the Georgia and South Carolina coast, known as the Sea Islands, to work on isolated plantations. In the days following the end of the Civil War, many of these ex-slaves were forgotten, but they continued to thrive, albeit provincially. The most significant aspect of their postwar existence is that they lived without measurable intrusion from the outside world. In short, they forged ahead as an intact African (American) community, maintaining cultural nuances and linguistic patterns from the distant past. Willow Springs might seem like a completely fictional place, but it does bear the stamp of reality given its connection to this historical truth.

Mama Day also borrows from African-American folklore in its rendering of the Day family history. Periodically alluded to throughout the novel is the history of Sapphira Wade, the great-grandmother of Mama Day and Abigail, who, after birthing seven sons to slave owner Bascombe Wade, somehow persuades Wade to deed the land to his progeny. No one is sure exactly how Sapphira accomplished such a feat. Some speculate that she even killed Wade after persuading him and then suddenly disappeared, perhaps on her way back to Africa. This part of the Sapphira Wade story is directly linked to the legend of Ibo Landing. In

1858 the slave ship *Wanderer* arrived on Ibo Landing, an island off the coast of Charleston, South Carolina. Myth suggests that as soon as the would-be slaves disembarked and saw their new home, they turned and proceeded to walk across the ocean on their way back to Africa, in a kind of reverse Middle Passage (the term applied to the slave journey from African shores to the Americas). Rituals of departure and return are a part of African (American) folklore. This legend serves in part as foundation of the history of African-American resistance and agency (the idea of taking action in one's life instead of accepting passively one's fate).

Willow Springs in general, and the Day family in particular, is created in the spirit of African-American agency. Because Sapphira Wade ensured an inheritance for her children, Willow Springs has been allowed to flourish in the present, largely free of outside (European) encroachment. Naylor alludes as well, though, to the harsh reality of African-American land ownership. While Willow Springs is still intact, its primacy has been threatened over the years by crafty and greedy developers. In the 1980s, when Naylor was in the throes of crafting this novel, unsettling stories were emanating from the coastal regions of Georgia and South Carolina concerning the plight of poor African Americans whose families had owned waterfront properties for generations (land gained largely because whites had formerly thought such land was worthless for agricultural purposes). Now that such land was deemed valuable as a place for the construction of resorts, these blacks were swindled out of their holdings, or if they refused to acquiesce, their taxes were summarily raised and because they could not afford to maintain payment, they lost land that developers then scooped up for a pittance. This is the harsh history that Naylor is also addressing. Willow Springs is a testament to what might have been.

In terms of literary history, one important predecessor is Pat Conroy's *The Water Is Wide*, an account of the author's brief tenure as a white schoolteacher on Yamacraw Island, one of the all-black Sea Islands off the coast of Beaufort, South Carolina. Conroy's is a paradoxical tale of one who wishes to provide the children with an education appropriate for the modern world but who also understands the cultural sacrifice made by his encroachment upon their lives. In addition, an immediate forerunner to *Mama Day* is Toni Morrison's *Beloved* (1987) and, remotely, the other works in Morrison's canon that predate *Beloved*. Like these Morrison novels, *Mama Day* employs magical realism, or speculative fiction, as a dominant genre. In such a work, the reader is presented with a changed, altered, or distorted reality in order to challenge his or her notions of the real and the known. Representation emerges as a concept more important than fixed reality. For example, in *Beloved*, the valid question is not, "Is Beloved a ghost?" or "Is she the child that Sethe murders years before?" Rather, the question is, "What does this illusory figure represent?" Likewise, in *Mama Day*, the question concerns not whether Mama Day is a conjure woman or if in the other place unnatural (or supernatural) events occur; rather the question concerns whether or not someone socialized in one perspective (one reality) can relinquish a single point of view (comfort zone) long enough to consider another point of view, especially if, as in the case of George, one's willingness involves the life of a loved one.

Such literature transcends time, space, and memory. And because fixed reality is not a given luxury, the reader is left to confront the unknown world without the benefit of normal sensory tools. As the narrative voice states about the story of Sapphira Wade, "[She] don't live in the part of our memory we can use to form words" (4). And according to George, "The clocks and calendars we had designed were incredibly crude attempts to order our reality. . . . All of those numbers were reassuring, but they were hardly real" (158).

In addition to her use of magical realism, Naylor also defers, if only briefly, to the futuristic novel. And while *Mama Day* is neither Utopian (a futuristic novel about an ideal imaginary world) nor Dystopian (a futuristic novel about a problematic imaginary world), it does acknowledge a future time. The George and Cocoa story technically ends with George's death in 1985, and the publication date for the novel is 1988, yet Naylor ends the novel in 1999. With this technique Naylor ponders possibilities far beyond what one knows in the present moment. Though Cocoa has moved on with her life and, to some degree, beyond the tragedy of George's death, she is still linked to that past, and in the same way, she is inextricably bound to an unknown future. Neither bad nor good, this future simply is. Just as Sapphira Wade's actions in 1823 set a course for the future of her family, so too will Cocoa's actions from 1985 on set a course for her sons and the progeny to follow thereafter.

NARRATIVE TECHNIQUE

Unlike her first two novels, which are structured around a series of ministories that collectively constitute the larger text, *Mama Day* focuses mainly on one major plot. In theory, then, the novel boasts a traditional linear format, but in reality Naylor manipulates the would-be chronological nature of the narrative movement in favor of a more original structure. After the prologue, the novel is divided into two sections: before Cocoa and George's visit to Willow Springs and then the events following their arrival on the island.

The prologue is narrated by one unifying voice that represents the people and the culture of the island. This voice provides the history of Willow Springs, particularly in regard to the Day family. Though set in 1999, with the narrative voice looking back not only on events from the extended past but also on the events to be chronicled in the novel's plot, the prologue recounts details from Willow Springs myth and legend as a means of establishing a cultural and a historical context, extending its time line from 1823 to 1999. This prologue also serves to show how the past is ever-present in the contemporary moment; in fact, it completely disturbs the notion of isolated moments in time. Instead, time is of a more fluid nature, with past merging with present and also with future.

As a means of underscoring this point, the narrative voice reveals the importance of 1823 as the year when the legend of Sapphira Wade (matriarch of the Day clan) is born. Different stories detail different methods she used to kill her master, Bascombe Wade, who is also the father of her seven sons, but not before he deeds his holdings to his mixed offspring. One story has her actually marrying him and then killing him after persuading him to will his land to her children. Other stories suggest that some of the sons are not Bascombe Wade's. Nevertheless, 1823 has gone down as a banner year in shaping the future of Willow Springs, in fact to such an extent that the present-day inhabitants of the island use "18 & 23" as a colloquialism, either as a verb or noun to indicate something unusual, unexpected, unacceptable, or potentially deceptive. Its meaning actually fluctuates to accommodate the context of the statement. In this way, the Sapphira Wade story is always active in the lives of Willow Springs denizens, if only indirectly.

The prologue also establishes the context for the novel's plot. The reader learns that Cocoa is now living outside Charleston with her second husband and two sons and that she now visits Willow Springs often to meet up with her first husband, who remained in Willow Springs after Cocoa left. She and her first husband, George, talk for over two hours during these visits. And it is one of these visits that serves as the narrative vehicle for the novel. Not until the end of the novel does the reader realize that George is dead and that Cocoa, in making these visits, must go to the cemetery.

After the prologue, the novel is narrated, with rare exception, intermittently by both George and Cocoa, each providing a perspective of their short life together. Each is ostensibly talking to (or thinking about) the other—sharing thoughts, feelings, frustrations, aspirations, disappointments, and joys, with George, of course, narrating from the grave. While there are no chapter breaks, interspersed throughout are section dividers. When neither George nor Cocoa is narrating, the collective voice of Willow Springs speaks, or Naylor uses extensive dialogue to convey the characters' thoughts. The bulk of the novel, with its focus on George and Cocoa, is set in the years between 1980 and 1985. Periodically the collective voice is inserted to offer a historical reference to the moment. (See Character Development and Thematic Issues sections.)

At the very end of the novel, Naylor returns to 1999, now with Cocoa looking back on the events of 1985 just prior to George's death. Fourteen years have elapsed, but Cocoa is still affected by her loss, though not as intensely as she was before. In the prologue the narrator, in explaining "18 & 23," recalls "that '18 & 23 summer' [when] the bridge blew down" (4), referring, of course, to the hurricane of 1985 that preceded George's death. In this way, 1823 is connected—spiritually, emotionally, and narratively—to 1985 and, by extension with Cocoa's remembrances, to 1999. In order to appreciate the comprehensive nature of these cross-generational ties and the open-ended structure of the narrative, it is important to recall that the publication date for *Mama Day* is 1988. This said, it is obvious that Naylor is extending the novel's story to the far-ranging future. Just as the Sapphira and Bascombe Wade stories are not fixed in a moment of time, neither is the George and Cocoa story. The imaginative world of Willow Springs lives on. The family chart that precedes the prologue reveals Sapphira's birth year as 1799, yet she is one who impacted the next century. Likewise, the events that Cocoa is recalling in 1999 will impact the following century. And the story (-ies) will live on. This thought is embodied in the title character who, in 1999, is still living. Abigail died in 1990, but Mama Day still thrives on at 104 and will probably live to witness the next century. Born in 1895 Mama Day is the spiritual and narrative connection (hence her importance as the title character) linking the nineteenth, and twentieth centuries, and more than likely, the twenty-first century. And with her bond to Sapphira Wade, she is retrospectively linked to the eighteenth century.

It is also important to note that with this third novel Naylor confirms an intertextual link among the works in her canon. With this technique Naylor shows how each novel is not just an entity unto itself. Rather, each novel's story is a part of a larger, more inclusive African-American story. No work, then, is a finite product. Each must be considered in response to yet another one. For example, Cocoa Day is the first cousin of Willa Prescott Nedeed, the wife of Linden Hills patriarch Luther Nedeed, both of whom suffer a tragic death at the end of *Linden Hills*. This tragedy occurs just one year before George and Cocoa begin dating in *Mama Day*. The reminder of this sudden death gives Cocoa all the more reason to consider marrying this man George with whom she initially thinks she has nothing in common. The mystery of what happened to the Nedeeds also affects Mama Day, but only to intensify her suspicions of urban life and northerners. The events presented in *Linden Hills* provide a backdrop for the ensuing events in *Mama Day*.

Similarly, Naylor also anticipates her fourth novel, *Bailey's Cafe*, while writing *Mama Day*. To some degree *Bailey's Cafe* is a prequel of *Mama Day*. George Andrews is born at the end of *Bailey's Cafe* and is turned over to the Wallace P. Andrews Home for Boys. In a heated argument just prior to his marriage to Cocoa, George reveals the fact that he was born in *Bailey's Cafe*. *Mama Day*, then, looks back to past events from *Linden Hills* while simultaneously looking back (in terms of narrative time) and looking forward (in terms of publication of text) to *Bailey's Cafe*. Hence, the second, third, and fourth novels are tightly woven together. Even *The Women of Brewster Place* and *Linden Hills* are linked, if only tangentially. Kiswana Browne of *The Women of Brewster Place* hails from the Linden Hills neighborhood, but as Willie and Lester observe in *Linden Hills*, she had sense enough to leave.

The narrative techniques that Naylor employs, then, are not reserved for whatever individual work she is crafting at the moment. Instead, she is developing a whole universe of characters who shed light on various aspects of the African-American experience. Her method of rejecting the linear narrative for any single work becomes even more understandable when one realizes that each work does not stand alone. Rather, each is connected to the other. And together they penetrate past, present, and future.

A PSYCHOANALYTICAL APPROACH

A helpful way of assessing this work is a psychoanalytical approach. And because the definitive scholar on modern psychology is Sigmund Freud (1856–1939, Austrian psychiatrist and founder of psychoanalysis), his concepts are the most useful. Freud observed that most people's conscious lives are troubled by unconscious fears or desires, often relating to childhood experiences. In order to help the patient escape this mental anguish, Freud invited the patient to talk freely about his or her childhood, dreams, and/or fantasies, whatever might yield insight into this unconscious mental territory. A secondary, but integral, component to this theory included Freud's notion that sexual energy (the most basic human force and the entire drive toward physical pleasure) caused the human mind much confusion, because such energy, as it stood in conflict with the mandates of a civilized society, was summarily repressed. Yet this repressed energy had to display itself somehow, if not in constructive ways, then in destructive ones. Sexual energy and childhood experience are also linked in Freudian theory. As a child's first sexual yearning is linked to the opposite-sex parent, according to Freud, these parent-child relationships are crucial to understanding the adult child's relationships with others.

A psychoanalytical reading of a literary work allows the student to investigate more thoroughly the conscious and subconscious motivations of key characters. This form of criticism provides the reader with tools for understanding the relationship between a character's feelings or mental state and the character's actions. Such an analysis can be indispensable in gauging character development. When relevant, a psychoanalytical critic might also be concerned with the author's motives and how such motives have affected the creation of characters and story line.

To some extent Naylor constructs her narrative around psychoanalysis. As George and Cocoa reminisce about their life together, they reevaluate every aspect of their journey together. The sections that they narrate read very much like journal entries, the effect of which is to heal former pains and frustrations. With this "free talk" method, both narrators reveal seemingly unconnected aspects of their individual personalities, only later to discover that these various components make up who they are, imperfect though each person is. Yet when they unite in matrimony these components create a complete unit. For example, what is lacking in Cocoa is compensated for in George, and vice versa. George's practicality helps to ground Cocoa, while her temperamental behavior constantly challenges him.

George and Cocoa fully appreciate their compatibility only after George is dead, however. During much of their short-lived marriage they challenge each other in ways they do not fully understand. As Freudian theory suggests, human behavior is linked to childhood issues. This is certainly the case with George and Cocoa. Each of them suffers from a sense of loss (of the parents they never knew). Because Cocoa has never had a consistent male presence in her domestic life (her father abandoned her mother before Cocoa was born), she exhibits a subdued anger about men, an anger borne out of feelings of insecurity that fuels erratic behavior in her adult interactions with them. In short, every man must pay for the mistake made by her father. Two important examples support this assertion: Cocoa's initial attempt to force George to choose between his love of Monday-night football and his love for her; and her apparent jealousy when George adapts so well to life in Willow Springs and gains the love and respect of her family. Whenever she is denied George's undivided attention, Cocoa transforms into the little girl whose emotional void was never quite satisfied. Such a conflict is presented in one of the most crucial scenes in the novel, marking the worst altercation of their married life. On the night of their arrival in Willow Springs, Mama Day and Abigail honor them with a reception. Before the guests arrive, Cocoa, feeling particularly anxious and insecure, asks George how she looks, a question that George thinks requires an honest answer. But because Cocoa wants to make a notable impression on her old friends, she needs ego stroking from George, not for him to tell her that her foundation is too dark. This is a particular blow to her ego because Cocoa has always been self-conscious about her skin color. Lighter than all of the other girls in Willow Springs, she was often referred to as a leper and made to feel freakish. So returning home now with a husband was to satisfy two purposes, one conscious and one subconscious. She wanted to prove to everyone that she could find a man who would find her attractive enough to marry; and subconsciously she is filling an emotional void that has plagued her for a lifetime.

Likewise, George is reacting in the present moment to issues extending to his childhood. Because he was raised in the structured, emotionless environment of a state shelter, George functions, as noted above, in a practical, undeviating way. For him, everything operates on logical principles. There is a solution to every problem. Yet George still needs his emotional hunger fed, which is evident in the fact that he constantly refers to the practical teachings of Mrs. Jackson, the matron of the shelter. George tries to convince himself that her methods were sufficient, but in reality some aspect of his development is missing. Because he never interacted with a sensitive, caring mother, George is less prepared for his relationship with Cocoa. Like Cocoa, he exhibits puerile behavior when he feels abandonment or neglect. Soon after George and Cocoa are married, Cocoa, one day while conducting her morning ablutions, moves George's heart medicine to make room for her toiletries, only to witness George react in a volatile manner. Because he storms out of the house for what Cocoa considers only a minor change in his life/routine, she fears that George will not fully accept her presence in the house, the biggest change of all. To Cocoa, George overreacted for what was, at best, only a slight offense. While she can understand the importance of his needing to locate his medicine, she cannot understand his brusk behavior since she moved it only a bit. But for George, now that he has finally found a woman to love, and who loves him, he does not want to witness even the slightest disregard for his feelings and needs. While he does have an actual heart ailment, it is also his metaphoric heart that ails.

As stated above, Freud argues that children's sexual awareness (and subsequent sexual and/or behavioral issues) is directly connected to their relationships with the opposite-sex parent. For the boy, according to Freud, early sexual awakening begins when the mother nurses the baby; her breasts become the objects of his sexual desire. As noted earlier, George is denied this interaction since he never knew his natural mother. And it is a phase of life that he misses. This assertion is made evident in an important scene presented soon after Cocoa and George's arrival in Willow Springs. While the two are having dinner one night with Cocoa's old friends Bernice and Ambush, the topic of naming babies emerges. Bernice, arguing that a child needs only its given name, not a nickname, unknowingly makes a faux pas: "My own mama never gave me no outside name but the one I was born with. And your mama didn't either, did she, George?" (201). Because Cocoa feels guilty for not ever having warned Bernice about George's mysterious parentage, she dreads George's later retaliation for this silent humiliation. Her fear, as she undresses for bed later that night, is that George will vindictively criticize the size of her breasts, an insecurity she has long harbored. But instead of attacking Cocoa in this way, George responds in a subtle, yet emotionally charged way. Cocoa describes their interaction after they are in bed: "Your face stayed turned and it was barely a whisper: I'd like you to nurse our children. I said nothing as I waited. The silence grew longer and longer. The silence stayed. You slipped under the covers, cradled your head between my breasts, and we never spoke about the tears" (202). Clearly, Bernice's question triggers an insecurity in George about his being denied any interaction/intimacy with his natural mother. And later with Cocoa, in a symbolic gesture, George yearns to be embraced in the bosom of a mother figure, this time Cocoa.

6

Bailey's Cafe
(1992)

Naylor's fourth novel, *Bailey's Cafe*, returns to the looser narrative structure noted in both *The Women of Brewster Place* and *Linden Hills*. Sketching the lives of a host of bizarre characters, this novel focuses on issues of marginality. Each of the characters, while visiting the title setting, is in transition, having barely escaped lives of not-so-quiet desperation in hopes of regaining direction and purpose. The unifying thread is the narrative voice of Bailey himself, the present manager of the cafe who, after relating his own trying tale, introduces the reader to various patrons whose individual life histories constitute the different chapter divisions. It is appropriately set in 1948, a period of significant transition in American history between the aftermath of World War II and the Civil Rights Movement to be ushered in with the 1954 Supreme Court ruling of *Brown v. the Board of Education of Topeka, KS*, which mandated school integration. Like these characters, the country is, to some degree, in limbo, having also shed its innocence in the throes of global war while yet uncertain about its ability, or even willingness, to move forward, particularly in regard to racial issues. In this compelling novel, Naylor offers a chance for both the country and her characters to mature and realize their utmost potential.

PLOT DEVELOPMENT

Like *The Women of Brewster Place* and *Linden Hills* Naylor's fourth novel is composed of several miniplots. Each chapter details the life struggle of a different character. From these collective stories the reader confronts once again the depths of human struggle and survival despite the odds. Bailey's Cafe serves as a sanctuary for those who have been forsaken or who have been denied the solace of human compassion. It is a way station where customers are left to their own devices without interference from others. They can interact if they wish, or they can sit quietly to contemplate their condition. Because the customers have been exploited either emotionally or physically, Bailey's offers them a place where they can try to function unmolested until they can figure out their next alternative.

One of the first characters to be introduced is Sadie, described as a wino, a whore, and a lady. Sadie has entered the cafe from the south side of Chicago, where she has maintained a life of quiet desperation. By the time she is ten, Sadie has become the house cook, seamstress, maid, cobbler, laundress, and general caretaker for an overbearing alcoholic mother. By the time Sadie is thirteen, her mother forces her into prostitution. And several months later, the mother subjects the young girl to a painful abortion, not only physically but also emotionally. By suggesting to Sadie that her life would have been much worse with a child, the mother is implying that her own life with Sadie has been a mistake. Despite her horrific home environment, Sadie fights to become a respectful lady, even though she is still a prostitute.

Sadie's mother dies when Sadie is fourteen, and with no visible means of support beyond prostitution, Sadie continues in that trade until she lands a job as cleaning woman at an upscale white brothel, soon becoming one of the house favorites. While working there, Sadie meets the man who will become her husband. Daniel, thirty years her senior, delivers firewood to the house once a week, and though he and Sadie barely exchange words in the three years that she works there, he extends a marriage proposal to her when he learns that the house has been closed down by law officials. For the next two decades Sadie functions as Daniel's wife and housekeeper, daunting tasks because he is silent to an extreme and the house is positioned near railroad tracks where coal-carrying train cars career by, leaving behind smoke clouds and coal dust.

Although Daniel does not seem to appreciate Sadie's efforts, she remains committed to creating a pleasant home life for herself and her husband. Having learned the art of invisibility from living with a stern mother, Sadie knows not to intrude on Daniel's space and consequently negotiates around him whenever he is present.

When Daniel dies after twenty-five years of marriage, Sadie is left with nothing. Because Daniel bequeathed the house to his two estranged daughters from a previous marriage, Sadie must try to raise money (in less than a month) in order to purchase the property, as neither daughter is willing to transmit the deed to Sadie. After searching endlessly, and unsuccessfully, for employment that will yield enough income to complete the purchase, Sadie is reduced once again to prostitution. But she is determined to sell herself for only the daily amount she has calculated she will need in order to meet the total amount by the end of the month. Though she has resigned herself to prostitution, she does not want to associate herself with the moral turpitude of prostitution. Her association extends from need only, not from degradation. When she tells her potential client that she requires only $2.04 (in order to meet her daily $5.79 goal; she has already earned $3.75) and proceeds to make change for him, he is both confused and amazed. Yet he, a plainclothesman, arrests her. And by the time Sadie exhausts her two-week stay in jail, she has no time to earn the full amount for the house.

Losing the house, Sadie removes to a women's shelter, only to lose her bed there because she refuses to accept public relief. Instead, Sadie becomes homeless, selling her body only when she needs food or liquor so that she can temporarily forget her troubles. It is from the street that she ventures into Bailey's Cafe and asks for a cup of tea. Even though Sadie has led a life of ill repute, Bailey recognizes Sadie's elegance and manners. While her circumstances may identify her, they do not fully define her.

Sadie's story in the cafe ends when she rejects the marriage proposal of the local ice deliveryman. Whenever Sadie visits the cafe, the local ice deliveryman joins her at the table and regales her with stories from his daily ritual. After a while, the two become friendly enough for Sadie even to venture a few words. But usually she just remains quiet, offering only a smile or a nod. On one evening, though, Iceman invites Sadie to dance with him on the pier adjacent to the cafe. When she acquiesces, Iceman takes the opportunity to propose, assuring Sadie that his pension will provide for both of them. Sadie, however, still reeling from past disappointments, declines, fearing future loss and frustration. Although she briefly fantasizes about a fulfilling life with Iceman, she ultimately decides that she would bring his life only pain and turmoil.

The next chapter belongs to Eve, who owns the boardinghouse (brothel) next door to the cafe. Eve is described as a peculiar and particular woman, who does not allow just any downtrodden woman to reside in her establishment. She provides sanctuary only to those women who truly need help or in whom she sees promise. Though both the cafe and the boardinghouse may be havens, only the cafe welcomes anyone.

Eve has arrived at Bailey's (or next to Bailey's) from New Orleans, where she amassed a fortune in the prostitution business after being cast from home in rural Louisiana. An orphan, Eve is raised by a stern minister, whom she calls Godfather. Her relationship with this man is strange at best, completely dysfunctional at worst. Even after she undergoes the early stages of puberty, Godfather is still laundering her personal items and giving her a nightly bath, much to the consternation of the local community. He ultimately stops the baths, but he still prevents her from socializing with other children, especially boys. While Eve recognizes that Godfather needed to discontinue the baths, she misses being touched by another human being. And as her body continues to grow and develop, she yearns for any kind of touch or stimulus. Soon she discovers a way to be satisfied, one that will ultimately wreak havoc on her home life with Godfather. Allowed only to play hide-and-go-seek with a mentally challenged boy named Billy, Eve invents another game that provides her with physical pleasure. Lying in a prone position, pressing her body into the ground, Eve instructs Billy to march back and forth around her body while stomping as vigorously as he can.

When Godfather discovers this "game," he, in outraged response, forces Eve to leave home. Unflappable, Eve journeys to New Orleans, where in ten years she develops a talent for making money and a love for well-kept gardens. Never subjecting her own body to prostitution, she sees herself as simply providing a service for a basic human need. Upon leaving New Orleans and finding herself next to Bailey's, Eve establishes her boardinghouse, outside of which she has created the loveliest of gardens. And from these gardens, she insists her tenants' "gentleman callers" purchase flowers to bestow upon their chosen "lady."

The remaining chapters focus on characters who wind up not just at Bailey's but also at Eve's, the first of whom is Esther. Forced into prostitution at age twelve, Esther remains in this condition for twelve more years. At the request of her older brother, Esther becomes the concubine of her brother's boss, a wealthy farmer who provides her with a comfortable house and plenty of food. And because her brother has a wife and eight children to feed, Esther agrees to what she thinks is marriage to the farmer. Remaining with the farmer for twelve years in order to pay her brother for each year that he cared for her, "against the shrill protests of [his] fat wife" (98), Esther is subjected to unspeakable sexual acts that the farmer insists she perform in the basement of the house. At age twelve, Esther is naive and does not understand that when the farmer encourages her to play with the toys he has purchased for her, he is introducing her to sexual toys and sexual games.

By the time she is twenty-four, Esther realizes, of course, that she is not legally married to the farmer. When she arrives at the boarding-house, Eve, understanding her past, provides her with a room in the basement, where she can hide in the darkness. All of her clients never see her in the light. She can function only in darkness. And because she forever feels cheated out of a proper wedding and marriage, she insists that her callers bring white roses, which she can faintly discern in the dark.

The next chapter focuses on Mary (a.k.a. Peaches), described as the most beautiful woman anyone has ever seen. When the chapter opens, Peaches' father has entered Bailey's Cafe in search of his daughter, who has taken up residence at Eve's house. Fully aware that Peaches is now living a life of ill repute, Daddy Jim wants to rescue Peaches and return her to Kansas City. However, Peaches' life has changed so much since she last lived in Kansas City that she cannot simply return so easily.

When Peaches was a young teenager living in her parents' home, the boys in the neighborhood often pursued her, but because her father was so protective, she was not allowed to date any of the prospective suitors. In an attempt to harness her own sexuality and repress any desire, Peaches ironically becomes controlled by an ever-intensifying urge. Seeing herself as two people, one pure, wholesome, and good, and the other wicked, promiscuous, and aggressive, Peaches decides to submit the lascivious one to a host of men in order to protect her more sacred self. Peaches is plagued by her beauty because men constantly flirt with her, accost her, or leer at her. Believing she has no other recourse, Peaches engages in one affair after the other. Soon she earns a reputation for loose behavior, much to the consternation of her father who, upon learning of a recent tryst, would seek revenge against the man.

Finding it difficult to see her father tormented in this way, Peaches ultimately leaves home, only to find herself living on the seedy side of town and prostituting in order to survive. Sinking lower and lower, Peaches begins to hate herself. Before, she found some peace in distinguishing between her good self and this wayward self. But now she sees her entire being consumed by sexual desire. By the time she is living with one man, who tries to save her in the way that her father did, she has lost all hope of rehabilitation. In an effort to rescue Peaches, her gambler boyfriend moves her from city to city, thinking that if she is removed from the source of her temptation (specific men), she will be strong enough to withstand the urges. Nothing, however, seems to remedy the situation.

Because Peaches feels guilty for her infidelity to this man, she makes a concerted effort to suppress her feelings. For two whole weeks, she refuses to leave their plush apartment, because she does not want to encounter any other men with whom she might be tempted to rendezvous. She even refuses to answer the door, lest she might seduce a deliveryman. And for two weeks she almost drives herself mad. It is at the end of the second week that she takes drastic measures. Believing that her beauty will forever plague her, Peaches takes a beer opener and slices a diagonal line across her right cheek all the way to the left side of her chin, all the while suffering piercing pain before passing out. Now that she is no longer beautiful Peaches feels relieved of the physical torment that has been a part of her entire life.

Upon her release from the hospital Peaches boards a train for no predetermined destination. She ultimately lands in Bailey's and is soon directed to Eve's where she has remained until the present. As the chapter ends, her father is sent to Eve's, but when he arrives there, Eve will not allow him to cross the threshold. Peaches remains at Eve's for now; at the very least, she knows that she can return home whenever she wishes.

Following Peaches' story is the saga of Jesse Bell, who has come to Eve's after surviving the deliberate sabotage of her happy domestic life. At Eve's she regains her equilibrium after suffering from an emotional downfall that leads also to drug abuse. Like the other women's stories, Jesse Bell's is a story of survival despite the obstacles placed before one. Jesse Bell hails from a solid working-class family and is proud of their fast-talking, hearty-living existence. Nevertheless, Jesse Bell marries into one of Manhattan's most prominent black families, the Kings. Unfazed by the King affluence and influence, Jesse Bell is simply happy to have found a man who seems to love her for who she is. And for a while, her life is fulfilling, particularly after the birth of her son, heir apparent to the King fortune.

Jesse Bell's marriage lasts for nineteen years, but signs of its demise emerge in the early years. Uncle Eli King, the family patriarch, has been determined from its inception to destroy the relationship, because he believes that Jesse Bell is not worthy of the King name. He accuses her of throwing veritable bacchanals wherein all sorts of lewd and lascivious behavior is condoned; he even suggests that Jesse Bell's elderly mother participates in such activities. And because of Uncle Eli's bourgeois pretensions, he disdains any conduct that, in his estimation, frames blacks in a stereotypical light. According to Jesse Bell, Uncle Eli was obsessed with "lifting" the black race to the level of (upper-class) white acceptance. Because of his obsession, Uncle Eli even criticizes the soul food that Jesse Bell prepares for her family, referring to it as slave food.

Ironically, many others in the King clan find Jesse Bell, her parties, and her food pleasing, often sneaking to Jesse Bell's house to enjoy her home cooking, that is, until Uncle Eli learns of the betrayal and admonishes the culprits. And while Jesse Bell suffers these various affronts to her dignity early in her marriage, it is not until after the birth of her son that matters worsen. Very subtly, but very methodically, Uncle Eli maneuvers himself into every important decision concerning the young King's life: what nanny to hire (instead of allowing Jesse Bell complete influence), what tutor to engage (instead of registering the boy for public school as his mother desired), or what camp to attend (instead of letting the boy go fishing with his Bell uncles). Yet when Jesse Bell alerts her husband to these machinations, he accuses her of being paranoid about his uncle. And because these intrusions "came in little pieces, one thing this year, another thing the next" (128), Jesse Bell cannot convince her husband of Uncle Eli's sinister intent. She only awakens one day to discover that her son has become a stranger to her and the other Bells, the day he refuses to attend her mother's ninetieth birthday party because "he didn't have anything in common with *those* people" (128).

The final blow comes to Jesse Bell on the day that the Kings celebrate her son's acceptance into Harvard. When Uncle Eli invites the Bells, Jesse Bell, justifiably suspicious of his motives, fears that only trouble can ensue. On the day of the cookout, it rains incessantly. Prepared, though, for this inclement weather, Uncle Eli readies the yard with a tent to protect his food and guests; however, he has told the Bells to arrive two hours later than the other guests so that by the time they do arrive, there is no more room available under the tent. As a consequence, the Bells cannot grill their food, because they cannot maintain a fire in the exposed open pit. Jesse Bell's mother catches a cold, which leads to pneumonia, and then she dies a month later. This turn of events completely unhinges Jesse Bell. But when her husband refuses to acknowledge that the whole scheme was premeditated, Jesse Bell seeks solace in the only friend she can ultimately trust—heroin.

Unfortunately for her, matters get even worse. When a lesbian club is raided, Jesse Bell, an affirmed bisexual, in attendance, is hauled off to a detention center. With the help of Uncle Eli her entire reputation is sullied in the local newspapers. And because her husband must protect the King name and legacy, he dissociates himself and his son from Jesse Bell. So Jesse Bell becomes an incarcerated junkie. Only when Eve, who visits the women's detention center periodically out of a sense of civic duty, discovers Jesse Bell and offers her the possibility of hope does Jesse Bell begin to recover from her devastating ordeal. This recovery is successful only after Eve employs tough love. Initially believing that Jesse Bell is incapable of beating her drug habit, Eve tests Jesse Bell's resolve by supplying her with as much heroin as she can ingest. After making Jesse Bell suffer through two bouts of painful four-day withdrawals, Eve finally believes that Jesse Bell is serious about her recovery. Jesse Bell's story ends with the hope that she will be strong enough to withstand temptation.

The chapter entitled "Mary (Take Two)" follows Jesse Bell's saga. It details the unbelievable story of a woman who is different from the earlier Mary (Peaches). To distinguish, Naylor calls this second character Mariam. With this chapter Naylor elevates the novel to a mystical plane, wherein Mariam assumes the central role in a tale of sacrifice and purity that challenges the reader's sense of reality and truth. Naylor also presents this chapter as a woman's story when she shifts the narrative voice from Bailey to his wife Nadine. As well, Eve shares in the retelling of Mariam's tale.

Mariam has come to live at Eve's house after having been thrust from her own country, Ethiopia, because others there believe she has sinned. An Ethiopian Jew, Mariam finds herself pregnant though she swears that she has never been with a man. Because she has such an innocent way about her, no one in the vicinity of Bailey's can question the veracity of her assertion.

Mariam is brought to Eve's by Gabe, the owner of the pawnshop that stands adjacent to the cafe. Gabe, who is also Jewish, is introduced in this chapter as a nemesis to Bailey. The two of them constantly argue over issues of race, history, politics, etc. That Gabe, a veritable curmudgeon, would assume responsibility for Mariam speaks well for Mariam's apparent innocence and virtue. Usually Gabe has nothing to do with Eve's establishment. Whenever transients happen into the pawnshop looking for sanctuary, Gabe sends them to the cafe, and then if Bailey sees fit, he will send them to Eve's. But for Mariam, Gabe makes direct contact, because he knows that given her predicament, Mariam will be treated with respect only at Eve's.

Much of the chapter details Mariam's life before she arrives at Eve's. While still young, Mariam had to undergo a rite of passage designed solely for girls, one to raise their value and increase their marital prospects. As a consequence, Mariam suffers genital mutilation (female circumcision). Because of her condition, according to Eve, there is no possible way that Mariam could have slept with a man without the knowledge of others, who would have heard her screams. Those in her village, however, believe Mariam to be lying, and when she refuses to name the father of her child, she is cast from the village. Journeying endlessly, she arrives in Addis Ababa, and from there, she finds Gabe's shop. Now, Eve and the others on the street must prepare for the birth of Mariam's baby.

Initially the other women (all the men, including Bailey, have left) in the cafe listening to this story are skeptical about Mariam's immaculate pregnancy. As a means of convincing them of Mariam's honesty, during Nadine's reexamination of Mariam's life, Eve showcases a truncated version of the ritual that Mariam suffered by using a plum. And though this display unnerves her audience, especially Nadine, Eve is determined to complete the ceremony and, to some extent, honor Mariam's courage and resilience. The women's squeamishness for what Mariam endured translates into a greater compassion for the young woman and an increased sensitivity not only for her past troubles but also for her present circumstances.

Naylor's longest and most comprehensive chapter, "Miss Maple's Blues," follows. Bailey resumes, at least briefly, his duty as narrator, his voice serving as transitional tool to link Miss Maple's self-narrated tale to the others. Miss Maple is actually Stanley, whose middle names are Beckwourth Booker T. Washington Carver, and who supplies no surname. Stanley is named after famous black men who contributed extensively to the betterment of American society, mainly because his father also wanted him to make his mark on society in an impressive way.

Stanley becomes Miss Maple after suffering a series of setbacks that left him unsure about his suitable place in America. Hailing from an impressive family who boast wealth, extensive landholdings, and a multicultural heritage, Stanley is destined to succeed in life. Growing up on the family ranch in rural southern California, Stanley is afforded privileges that few of any race in the first half of the twentieth century could claim. His father bestows upon him a private education and supplies him with as many intellectual challenges as Stanley can surmount. In short, his father prepares him to be his own man, though Stanley would not appreciate these efforts until much later.

Upon leaving home Stanley attends Stanford University where he pursues a degree in mathematics, ultimately earning his Ph.D., but not before he is drafted. Refusing, however, to fight for a country that does not consider him a full-fledged citizen, Stanley declines, opting instead to serve his time in jail as a conscientious objector. This rebellious nature will be vital in his transformation from Stanley to Miss Maple.

After completing graduate study Stanley sets out to secure gainful employment, firmly believing that with his credentials, with a post–World War II booming economy, and with the marketing analyst field burgeoning, he will successfully land a job. From Los Angeles to Philadelphia Stanley applies at various firms, only to be told that he could assume a blue-collar position but never an executive seat. Even though some interviewers are visibly disappointed that they cannot hire a perfectly qualified candidate, no one is willing to risk hiring a black man. Continuing to travel from west to east during an increasingly hot summer, Stanley soon discovers that he cannot abide the stifling men's clothing that he has worn for these various interviews. He then decides to don less restrictive, loose-fitting women's clothes, figuring that his chances of landing a job thus attired could not be any worse than they have been thus far.

Never securing that much sought-after job, Stanley (now Miss Maple) finds himself working as a housekeeper at Eve's. And because he feels freer, or as he indicates, "I'd never felt more like a man" (204), he continues to wear women's clothes during the warmer months. It is Eve who bestows upon him the title Miss Maple. Living at Eve's for two years now, Miss Maple has ironically amassed a small fortune by entering and winning jingle-writing contests sponsored by some of the very companies that refused to hire him. He uses the market research he performed in preparation for those interviews to assist him in crafting the perfect jingle. His story ends with the hope that he will be able to start his own company and finally chart his own course.

In the final chapter, entitled "The Wrap," Bailey attempts to conclude what has been an unconventional story. But because the overall text allows only a glimpse into the lives of the various characters, constructing a neat package at the end is all but impossible. Bailey does, however, allow in this final chapter greater insight into his love-hate friendship with Gabe, the Russian Jew. As stated above, the two men enjoy arguing about political and social issues, with each one vying for authority. According to Bailey, what makes their interaction special is the unconditional respect they have for each other. They dare to plumb topics that others of different backgrounds would never consider broaching. Nevertheless, when they discuss issues that are very personal to one of them, the other defers to the opinion/perspective of the first.

Nevertheless, it is from this position of mutual respect that Gabe and Bailey, and the others who frequent the cafe, attempt to help Mariam as she prepares for the birth of her child. As a black and a Jew, Mariam has by virtue of her very existence earned the loyalty of both men. Each of them tries to find a solution to Mariam's plight. Gabe seeks passage for her to Israel, but her entrance is denied. Bailey hopes that one of his customers might take her under wing and care for her and her child, but no one comes forward to assist. Soon after she delivers her robust son, Mariam dies, so the only recourse is to hand over the child—named George—to a shelter for homeless boys, managed by one of Bailey's acquaintances. The ending is neither happy nor sad; it is just matter-of-fact. In answer to what he argues is as realistic a conclusion as he can muster, Bailey submits, "I don't believe that life is supposed to make you feel good, or to make you feel miserable either. Life is just supposed to make you feel" (219).

CHARACTER DEVELOPMENT

In a novel that identifies several characters as significant, no one character tends to dominate the narrative. Since the reader is given mainly a sketch of each character's life, as in *The Women of Brewster Place* and *Linden Hills*, it is challenging to chart the comprehensive development of any one of them. Each character, in an individual way, represents a work-in-progress, for each is attempting to transform some important aspect of his or her life in order to gain, at the very least, a modicum of power and control. This tentative development is best described as a process whereby characters strive initially to please others (society, authority figures, etc.); then, finding such an attempt unsatisfying or unrewarding, they opt to please only themselves. Ultimately, however, with rare exception, they try to strike a balance between these two alternatives.

The key to understanding and appreciating the plight of these characters is Bailey who, along with his wife Nadine, recounts the stories of these transients with a matter-of-fact directness that both invites and commands respect for each of Eve's residents/Bailey's customers. Even the most bizarre tales are presented in such a way that the dignity of the "protagonist" is retained. Bailey soon alerts the reader that the world of the cafe is special and that the customers are to be accorded the same level of respect as one would extend to any human being. One must simply accept them as they are, just as one must accept the cafe, with its attendant rules, just as it is. While Bailey will not coddle the customers, just as he will not coddle the reader, he will allow them enough space to exorcise whatever demons are haunting them. With Bailey, as with Nadine, there is neither pretense nor hypocrisy.

This direct approach to life and to people, with little regard for foolhardiness, is best examined in Bailey's response to new customers who, unaware of the ordering policy, venture into the café. In Bailey's there are no entrée options during the week, only the standard fare for that particular day. However, on the weekends customers may order whatever they would like. Because some newcomers are perplexed by such choices, they will challenge the rule and place a far-fetched order. If the customer eats the strange food combination, it is free; however, if he refuses, Bailey makes sure the smart aleck pays for the trouble.

Like Bailey, Nadine is a no-nonsense person, who may or may not serve any given customer, depending on her temperament on that day. And Nadine refuses to observe standard rules of expected social behavior. When she and Bailey are dating just prior to their marriage, Nadine rarely exudes any excitement or pleasure about the courtship, if in fact it could be defined as such. On one occasion Bailey questions her about not having smiled all day, fearing that she might not be pleased with the date, and in response Nadine offers a question of her own: "But what does that [smiling] have to do with being pleased?" (17). Nadine rejects any prescribed notions of how she should behave or how she should respond to circumstances. Instead she charts her own course. A woman of few words, she chooses them carefully and utters them forcefully, fully expecting the listener to understand not only the words themselves but also the implied context.

Bailey and Nadine are the narrative voices through whom the reader is introduced to the other characters. With their somewhat implacable demeanor, they serve as protectors of these castaways whose vulnerabilities are heightened in their efforts to regain sanity and/or equilibrium in their lives as they undergo the developmental process noted above. No story presents this fact more clearly than does Sadie's. The only person whom Nadine actually serves twice (that in itself makes this customer a unique type), Sadie, while described as a whore and a wino, is also a lady. Because she is not easily categorized, one must simply accept her in her totality.

Sadie's life has been fraught with pain. For most of her years, she has attempted to please all others, first her mother (who never wanted to have children and who constantly referred to Sadie as The One The Coat Hanger Missed), then her husband (a taciturn man old enough to be her father who relished nothing but peace and quiet). In order to please both of them, Sadie elevates silence to a fine art; with her mother she softens a cracker in her mouth rather than chew it, lest she crunch too loudly and disturb her mother's drunken slumber. And with her husband Daniel, she sews peacefully while even timing herself to bite the thread at the same instant when Daniel clinks the ice in his whiskey-filled glass. Even when Sadie works as a maid in a brothel after the death of her mother and before her marriage, her job is to honor the requests of the residents and customers.

After being thrust from her home after the death of Daniel, Sadie seeks personal peace by periodically sipping tea alone in the cafe, the only apparent joy left in an otherwise forlorn life. However, during a brief phase, Sadie seeks a shred of joy for herself when she accepts the attentions of Iceman Jones, who tries so desperately to bring happiness to Sadie. For the first time in her life, Sadie seeks pleasure just for herself, and she seems to gain a measure of self-esteem. At one point she even fantasizes about embarking on a new life with Iceman. Unfortunately, the fantasy is short-lived, with Sadie ultimately rejecting Iceman's proposal and resuming her life on the street. At the very least, though, Sadie enjoys, if only temporarily, the company of a man who accepts her just as she is. And in terms of the developmental process, Sadie returns to her former life with something she never before enjoyed, unconditional love.

As with Sadie, Jesse Bell also spends the greater portion of her life trying to curry favor with others, in this case with her in-laws, the Kings. Devoting herself entirely to her husband and her son, Jesse Bell tries to prove that she is worthy of the King name by becoming a loyal wife and doting mother. As a consequence, she is practically blindsided when husband and son are taken from her. This "theft," at the hands of Uncle Eli, serves aesthetically to flesh out Jesse Bell's character. Because she is presented initially as a shrewd, streetwise person, one does not expect her to be easily duped. And in some measure, she is not. However, Jesse Bell is quite unprepared for the ensuing events that completely alter her life. Ironically, because she does falter, she is presented as a more complex character. The fact that she suffers makes her even more human (thus, vital) than she was before.

Jesse Bell's desire to be accepted by the Kings completely blinds her to the fact that she will never be accepted, that indeed she will be destroyed. In fact, the very person she thinks will usher her into full acceptance will be the one used to sever her ties with the family—her son. Recounting Uncle Eli's proud response to the boy's birth, Jesse Bell recalled thinking that this reaction signaled her own acceptance. Years later Jesse Bell will review this moment regretfully when she admits that she "shoulda listened more closely to what Uncle Eli was saying: Look what Jesse Bell has given *us*" (Naylor's emphasis; 127). That she, of all people, would miss the import of Uncle Eli's comment is a testament to her capacity for human imperfection, the depths of which mark her as a character primed for further growth and change.

Jesse Bell, after losing all that was precious to her and after almost losing her entire self, will create a new being once she becomes as devoted to herself as she previously was to the Kings. This devotion will entail, of course, her battling the drug addiction and suffering through the pains and pangs of withdrawal. By the time she is a veteran resident at Eve's, Jesse Bell has become her own person, no longer beholden to any authority but herself. When Bailey introduces her story, she has come by for one of her midnight card-playing games with him, defying Eve's curfew in an honest attempt to retain control over her life.

In addition to Sadie and Jesse Bell, Stanley (a.k.a. Miss Maple) emerges as the final well-developed character. Unlike Sadie and Jesse, however, Stanley is introduced as a defiant person, instead of one who must grow into rebellion. His development, then, entails honing his skills of resistance and learning to manipulate societal rules to his benefit. The very existence of Stanley and his family is a defiant act. As an affluent family of color (theirs is a mixture of ethnicities, not just African American), they challenge preconceived notions about the laziness associated with blacks, while Stanley's academic success challenges notions of inferiority. Later in life, Stanley will even rebel against his country when he assumes the posture of conscientious objector during World War II.

The real test for Stanley is presented, however, when he, now holding a Ph.D., pursues employment in corporate America. To most of these prospective employers, Stanley's presence is audacious. And when he refuses to accept positions less prestigious than those for which he is qualified, they consider him the epitome of arrogance, especially when he declines a job as "assistant to the assistant foreman" (202), or in the instance when he challenges the interviewer. Ultimately feeling disenchanted and utterly exhausted, Stanley finds himself in Bailey's, contemplating buying a revolver and a single bullet. The formerly strong, determined, undaunted Stanley seems completely defeated. This is a crucial turning point for one who has personified resistance. Stanley's growth, then, will come as a result of learning to recoup his strength and redouble his efforts not only to survive, but also to thrive in a world that would rather he fail.

By now Stanley has perfected the art of defiance. As Miss Maple, he rejects prescribed gender definitions. He is still a man though dressed in women's clothes. He is not a homosexual, and he does not want to be a woman. He is simply being himself with little or no regard for outside opinions. And as a means of truly perfecting his art and of gaining revenge, Stanley has manipulated the corporate system and, as a bonus, has made himself a wealthy man. By entering jingle-writing contests for various products, Stanley, who as a marketing research analyst—though unworthy of employment—studied America's postwar cultural wave, has amassed a small fortune. In short, he has used what he learned on those ill-fated interviews to tap the corporate coffers. And having successfully made such an inroad, he is now schooled on the true purpose and function of the contests. These arbitrary contests are not designed to reward talent. Rather, they are created to gauge the thought processes of the consumers so that the new slogans will then reflect these consumer thoughts/desires and result in higher sales. That a black, Ph.D.-holding transvestite brothel housekeeper has become financially successful at the expense of corporate greed is the ultimate defiant act and represents Stanley's continued intellectual development. Like the other characters discussed above, Stanley will use his knowledge to help himself, by pursuing his original goal of establishing his own business (he had planned to work in other companies only temporarily).

Significant minor characters include Sugar Man, Sister Carrie, Mr. and Mrs. Van Morrison, Uncle Eli, Miss Maple's father, Gabriel, and Daniel. Sugar Man is the area pimp and hustler whose main task is to entice wayward young women to work for him as prostitutes before they find their way to Eve's brothel. He is presented as the ultimate human parasite who not only feeds off of the misery and misfortune of others but also denigrates others in a futile effort to define himself. This attempt is made clear in Sugar Man's treatment of Miss Maple. Even though Bailey has repeatedly told him that Miss Maple is not gay, Sugar Man needs to relegate Miss Maple to homosexuality in order to keep himself sane and his own world "normal." He must place, or "fix," others to make himself comfortable. Ostensibly presented as his opposite is Sister Carrie, resident Bible-thumper and self-righteous voice of morality. She is, however, just as despicable as Sugar Man. Sister Carrie patronizes the cafe only to secure an audience for her endless harangues on the mortal and venial sins of everyone but herself. She is especially insulted that Bailey would serve anyone who lives in, or is in any way connected with, Eve's house. Sister Carrie cannot see herself and the patrons as human; she can be human only if she re-creates them as subhuman. But because Bailey's, the world that Naylor has created, welcomes difference, Sister Carrie is presented only as a carping and shrewish woman. Even though she vies so desperately to be the authority on righteousness and normalcy, Sister Carrie emerges, ironically, as marginal to the marginalized, and as a consequence, ultimately she has no authoritative voice in the novel. Mr. and Mrs. Van Morrison are the couple for whom Bailey's parents worked when he was a young boy. Affluent blacks, they made Bailey's family feel inferior and beholden. Striving too desperately to be accepted into white society, they fail to acknowledge their own oppressive behaviors in their interaction with less affluent blacks.

Similar to the Van Morrisons is Uncle Eli, in-law to Jesse Bell and catalyst for her downfall. Because he, too, is obsessed with elitist values, he demeans those blacks who, he believes, are inferior to him. Still another minor character who has achieved economic success yet has not allowed it to consume him (at least not in regard to other blacks) is Stanley's father. As a wealthy landowner and businessman, he has tried to instill in Stanley (a.k.a. Miss Maple) a sense of pride in the family accomplishments, particularly in the face of white bigotry. Gabriel, Russian Jew and pawnshop owner, provides the means of challenging arbitrary social and religious boundaries. Though Gabe and Bailey are often at odds in any political or religious discussion, they ultimately find common ground, even if they merely agree to disagree. Gabe's presence, and his interaction with Bailey, reminds the reader that "differences" must somehow coexist. Daniel, Sadie's husband, is important because he prods the reader to assess even the most minor characters as comprehensively as possible. On the surface a bitter and distant man who offers Sadie no emotional support, Daniel is, in fact, a man with feeling. The reader glimpses this depth only when Daniel, drunk and despondent, mutters about lifelong frustrations and offenses he has suffered. With each utterance the reader discovers that Daniel's manhood and humanity have been systematically eroded over time.

THEMATIC ISSUES

While Naylor tackles many different topics in *Bailey's Cafe*, the one theme that consumes much of the work is marginality. In every aspect, and on every level of the novel, Naylor explores the idea of defying boundaries and discarding labels. From the characters she chooses to create to the circumstances she crafts for them, Naylor embraces marginality as a suitable condition for real people who lead real and poignant lives. As the original dust jacket for the novel states, Bailey's Cafe "is a magnet that draws a wide variety of society's detritus." That Naylor would write an entire novel that addresses the plight of the downtrodden shows an appreciation for those who are, and for that which is, decidedly different. Peopling this drama is a transvestite, a heroin addict, a bordello owner, a wino (and prostitute), and a nymphomaniac, among others. Each, however, has an important story to tell, one that taps into the pain of human suffering and touches the heart of all who hear it. Though they may be called misfits when perceived from an assumed position of normalcy, within the confines of the work each is as normal as his or her circumstances allow. In short, Naylor forces the reader to (re-) consider these characters only in the context of their individual lives.

As a means of highlighting this notion of marginality Naylor sets the story in a mythical place. Bailey's is no ordinary cafe. Sitting "right on the margin between the edge of the world and infinite possibility" (76), the cafe represents the marginalized people who inhabit it. Like those people, the cafe is relevant and necessary. In short, it has a purpose.

Instead of being fixed in a particular city (the New York location, notwithstanding), the cafe is "real real mobile" (28). Every regular patron who first arrives enters the cafe directly from whatever city he or she has just departed, that is, from whatever place has caused the most recent pain, confusion, or despair. For Bailey himself, it is San Francisco. For Eve, it is New Orleans. For Sadie, it is Chicago. For Peaches, it is Cincinnati. For Mariam, it is Addis Ababa. And for Miss Maple, it is Pittsburgh. Since the cafe itself is rooted in no particular place, it is the perfect haven for its transient patrons.

Once inside the cafe, one must quickly learn to interpret the subtleties of the place. Bailey points out that in the cafe and beyond, "most of what happens in life is below the surface" (19). In these observations Bailey emphasizes that one must be open to possibilities. People who enter the cafe with preconceived notions (i.e., with fixed boundaries, labels, and rigid ideas of reality, all to be equated with a "surface" understanding) will miss the bulk of the information to be communicated. To function on the surface is tantamount to remaining beholden to one's own sense of the real, or one's own perspective. This self-deception emerges as a secondary theme. Yet Bailey (and consequently, Naylor) asks, why bother with the journey if one does not intend to grow and learn from the experience?

Everyone who enters the cafe is in transition. Life in the real (or other) world has become overwhelming, unfair, and even cruel. In the "transitional space" of the cafe, customers can relax unmolested as they attempt to regain composure. In celebrating marginal people who find themselves in a marginal place, Naylor also celebrates (in fact, urges) the possibility for change. Because pat labels and simple clichés are insufficient in identifying the characters or in describing their lives, none of them is left in a fixed, static condition. Rather their lives are nebulous, their futures ambiguous. They have achieved a peaceful limbo, and because of their apparent resilience and adjustability, they will more likely grow and develop in ways far beyond those who are settled in a comfortable, pigeonholed existence.

As a means of further foregrounding this transitory ideal, Naylor even questions Bailey's identity. Bailey is not really Bailey. The present proprietor of the cafe, whom the reader calls Bailey, simply adopted the name that was already sketched on the outside of the cafe when he assumed ownership. Eschewing a fixed label because he believes it insufficient in capturing the complexity of his identity, "Bailey" would rather allow latitude for self-definition.

Naylor's attention to marginality provides the appropriate prelude to yet another significant theme, establishing and maintaining respect for others' reality. Because all of the characters are, or have been, in some way marginalized or persecuted, they better appreciate the oppression of others. Instead of an oppressed person becoming the oppressor of another, these characters are so focused on trying to regain their own equilibrium, they cannot fathom the notion of trying to survive or thrive at the expense of another's pain, or attempting to glorify their own trials by belittling the struggle of another. In discussing his interactions with Gabe, Bailey echoes this sentiment: "We don't get into comparing notes on who did what to whom the most. Who's got the biggest pile of bodies. The way I see it, there is no comparison" (220). In other words, Bailey allows Gabe his reality, while Gabe does likewise.

Naylor's attention to marginality (defying boundaries and restrictions) and to respecting others' reality segues to an equally important and related theme: understanding that reality is a carefully designed, albeit arbitrary, construct. Simply put, those with political and economic might have the power to define social (i.e., the standard) reality, but one's individual sense of reality is provided by personal experience along with its cultural foundation. However, when the minority reality (experience) collides with that of the majority, the minority's worldview is rejected as either distorted or nonexistent. Jesse Bell's tale is one that illustrates this point. Even though her former life is systematically ruined by Uncle Eli, who drives her to the point of such distraction that she seeks relief in the only source available to her, heroin, Uncle Eli, powerful and well-connected, can determine exactly how the King family tragedy will be recorded (historicized). His account will emerge as the "truthful" (or real) version. Imagining what this version will be, Jesse Bell laments, that "it's all about who's in charge of keeping the records, ain't it?" (118). And those in charge of the records have the authority to determine the contents of those records.

This same issue is at the heart of a major conflict in Stanley's (Miss Maple's) early life. During his formative years, Stanley often resented the fact that his father would taunt the local whites with his wealth and acquisitions yet would refuse to fight like a man whenever he was challenged. For this reason, Stanley assumes his father is weak, when, in fact, his father simply refuses to acknowledge white primacy; to him most whites are merely invisible. As his father warns, "to accept even a single image in their language as your truth is to be led into accepting them all" (182). Stanley's father does not want his son to believe, in this case, that white reality (with its presupposition of white supremacy and black bestiality) should define his self-perception. Whites may control the information and the ideas broadcast, but Stanley should in no way adopt these perceptions as his own. Instead, he must create a language and a set of standards that make his reality the norm. To depend on the language of the majority to define the minority leads to self-destruction, since, of course, the majority has no suitable means of positioning, in this case, black normalcy. Recalling the difficulty that the whites in the vicinity had in comprehending the economic success of his family's ranch, Stanley understands that these onlookers could not reconcile the idea of Stanley's family, whom they considered subhuman, and American success assuming the same space. Such a concept is beyond the scope of their reality. Nonetheless, it is Stanley's responsibility to reject their perspective and to create a language (if only known to him) to verify himself, not for others but for his own emotional peace.

Naylor's focus on marginality is a deliberate attempt to reestablish a commitment to the inclusion of all kinds of people to whatever the discussion. As a means of succeeding in this goal, Naylor must also impel her readers to question their understanding of what is normal or standard. No better example of this challenge exists than Bailey's attitude concerning the holiday season; he refuses to decorate for a Christian holiday that would exclude so many people. Of course, a largely Christian country like America assumes that Christianity is the standard religion or, if not, that it should be. Bailey puts the reader on notice that such a perspective is quite arrogant given the reality of the global numbers. It is this kind of awareness that Naylor tries to effect. Naylor blends several themes—marginality, change and transition, and respect for others' reality (point of view)—in an effort to encourage compassion and sensitivity for difference.

HISTORICAL CONTEXT

Bailey's Cafe is set in 1948, the post–World War II period that marked an important crossroad not only in American and African-American history, but also in global history. While segregation was still the law of the land in America, 1948 ushered in an era of change, one that would culminate in the Civil Rights Movement of the 1950s and 1960s. However, the activism that marked the Movement would be a long time coming. Nevertheless, that Naylor has set her novel in 1948 is appropriate for a work that has as a thematic impulse new beginnings. Such beginnings, or the question of beginnings, are also relevant to Jewish exiles and survivors of the Holocaust. And with the 1948 establishment of Israel as a sanctuary for persecuted Jews, more questions than answers would develop.

One of the most notable occurrences in 1947 was the initial desegregation of major league baseball with Jackie Robinson joining the Brooklyn Dodgers. However, for someone like Bailey who only three years prior departed a segregated armed forces, the prospects for true American integration seem few. For him, Jackie Robinson's acceptance into professional baseball is not enough. In Bailey's opinion true integration would come only when blacks also owned, managed, and coached teams. That is, America would provide for her black citizens equal access to all elements of prosperity. In short, America would act American. But until this national character is actually realized, no true progress will occur.

In order to showcase widespread and repetitive human oppression, Naylor links the plight of blacks in America with that of the Holocaust survivors by presenting the issue of exile. Both groups suffered forced removal and were later denied freedom of movement. This post–World War II period, however, is a time of trying to reestablish boundaries, both literally (evident in the creation of Israel out of the former Palestine) and figuratively (evident in the attempt to renegotiate the boundaries of acceptable social interaction in regard to black-white exchange). Naylor introduces as one of her central characters Mariam, an Ethiopian Jew, who upon arriving at the cafe burdens Bailey, his wife, and others with the question of what to do with her. Mariam's presence in the novel allows Naylor to exploit this notion of marginality and force a discussion/analysis of identity and place. In some ways, Mariam, "a little snip of a girl bringing a really big question . . . because she got herself born black and a Jew" (221), is the quintessential exile. Like American blacks her identity is compromised when she is denied a place where she is fully accepted. Like Russian Jews she needs to find a place to call home. But as a black and a Jew, her very existence plagues those who cannot easily define her.

NARRATIVE STRUCTURE

Naylor relies on individual stories to present an overall narrative about the woes of the downtrodden. Each chapter is a complete unit, detailing the life of a different character. What unifies these stories is the presence of the main narrator, Bailey himself. His voice serves as the link among those in this bizarre cast. First narrating his own story, providing the reader not only with details of his childhood and military career but also with glimpses into his early life with his wife Nadine, Bailey then introduces the ensuing chapters, most often however relinquishing the storytelling responsibility to a particular character. In this way, then, Bailey's voice frames the voices of the other characters, by introducing and concluding the chapter (one exception is the chapter on Mariam, which Nadine narrates).

Time is an element that Naylor carefully manipulates, employing both linear (or traditional) and virtual (or flexible) time. Because Bailey's is a virtual (or mobile) cafe, appearing in whatever city a character needs to find a sanctuary, time becomes quite a relative concept. When a given character is telling his or her story, the narrative adopts whatever time period in the past the story dictates, never extending more than a few years. In terms of linear time, the overall narrative proceeds from the summer of 1948 to the summer of 1949, from the time Bailey introduces the first story until he presents the conclusion. Details like the holiday season and the mention of winter alert the reader that linear time has elapsed. By employing both elements of time, Naylor creates a more realistic work, even though she is presenting some rather unbelievable information. On the one hand, life moves along a chronological plane, as organisms move from inception to death. On the other hand, life (at least, human life) is consistently impacted by past events, a circumstance that makes these events a staple of the present. One of the overriding issues in this work is the extent to which these characters' past lives continue to impinge on their present concerns. By using this technique Naylor allows for a unified approach to her assessment of the novel's inhabitants.

As a means of accommodating this relaxed use of time, Naylor crafts the work as though it were an ongoing musical improvisation. The text becomes almost a moving, living piece, beholden to the whim of the immediate narrative voice (or singer). Many of the chapter headings help to illustrate this improvisational technique, for example, "Maestro, If You Please" (the opening chapter that introduces Bailey as prime narrator), "The Vamp" (one definition of *vamp* is "an improvised musical accompaniment"), "The Jam" (a section heading), "Mood: Indigo," "Eve's Song," and "Miss Maple's Blues." And in the opening chapter, Bailey prepares the reader/audience with the following: "There's a whole set to be played here if you want to stick around and listen to the music" (4). Using this device of improvisation, Naylor ironically creates a more realistic text (ironic in the fact that she addresses unusual issues, which might not be labeled realistic by some), because the result is a less contrived overall structure. The narrative disorder, or dissonance, is consistent with real-life movement. As Bailey states in the last chapter, "If life is truly a song, then what we've got here is just snatches of a few melodies" (219). And as with musical improvisation, both the composer and the listener participate in the ultimate interpretation. In this way, the novel is open rather than closed.

One of the most significant facets of its openness, or textual flexibility, is the novel's link to *Mama Day*. George, who is born to Mariam at the end of *Bailey's Cafe*, is presented as Cocoa's husband in *Mama Day*, Naylor's third novel and the predecessor to *Bailey's Cafe*. In this maneuver Naylor has not only bridged two different textual plots, but also manipulated yet again the element of time, splicing the 1940s time period of *Bailey's Cafe* with the 1980s and 1990s period highlighted in *Mama Day*. In so doing, Naylor nudges the reader beyond the parameters of a single text as a means of echoing her apparent assertion that no person, no text, no circumstance is a fixed, or static, entity. Consequently, each encounter must be considered with appropriate comprehensiveness.

In regard to literary prototypes, Naylor models *Bailey's Cafe* after Geoffrey Chaucer's *The Canterbury Tales*, successfully bridging the African-American and European literary traditions and disregarding, in yet another context, formerly imposed boundaries of separation. In Chaucer's work the pilgrims gather at Harry Bailly's Tabard Inn to embark on a spiritual journey during which they share tales to ease the passage of time. In Naylor's novel, however, Bailey's is a virtual cafe (though ostensibly located somewhere in Manhattan) that patrons enter from whatever city has most recently persecuted them. And, Bailey is not the actual name of the proprietor, though he agrees to accept the name since it was left painted on the establishment when he assumed his duties. While Chaucer's characters depart from and return to the Tabard Inn,

Naylor's characters find themselves in the cafe when they are most in need of sanctuary. And like Chaucer's, Naylor's "pilgrims" hail from every social and/or economic echelon.

A DECONSTRUCTIONIST READING

Deconstruction, as a method of literary criticism, strives mainly to uncover the ambiguities, contradictions, and ironies in a given text. This school of thought emerges out of the belief that language itself is inherently imperfect; consequently, meaning is arbitrary. Deconstruction analyzes the language to find the meaning below the surface. According to renowned theorist Ferdinand de Saussure there can be no fixed, known, or stable relationship between a word (symbol, or signifier) and the object (or signified) to which the word supposedly refers. For Saussure, the relationship is purely arbitrary, as imperfect human beings have assigned meanings to words as a means of trying to communicate, but there is no natural, or inherent connection. For example, *cat* has no real connection to the feline creature it conjures up in our minds. And to be sure, in another language a different symbol would attempt to call up the same object or image.

If language is imperfect in this way, says the deconstructionist, then whole texts composed of this flawed language are also subject to faults. It is the task of the deconstructionist to expose these various gaps, contradictions, ambiguities, and ironies. Mark Twain's famous protagonist and title character, Huck Finn, lends himself to deconstructionist critique and provides a general analysis. Young Huck is the embodiment of contradiction. On the one hand, he functions as a friend to freedom-seeking Jim. On the other hand, Huck is still influenced by a racist, slave-holding society that would rather see Jim dead than free. Throughout the novel Huck vacillates from one opinion to the other, seeming for some readers to be confused and inconsistent. However, the deconstructionist reader would find Huck's contradictions not problematic, but relevant as they unmask a truth about the society that has shaped Huck. The slave-holding society, too, is fraught with contradiction and ambiguity. It simultaneously espouses civility while engaging in barbarism. The deconstructionist would also critique the use of *slave* in reference to Jim. Though Jim is called a slave, he does not behave like a slave (he believes he deserves to be free). In fact, *slave* best describes the actual slaveholders, who are "enslaved" by a system that suppresses their own humanity,

a circumstance quite evident in their very act of slave-holding. A deconstructionist analysis allows the reader to assess more fully some of the
subtleties and ironies Twain is exposing about antebellum America.

Deconstructionist theory is helpful in analyzing *Bailey's Cafe* but not in
the typical way. Usually the critic, or theorist, would strive to uncover
the contradictions, or inconsistencies, in the actual text, or narrative. But
in the case of this novel, understanding deconstruction aids in understanding what Naylor is trying to accomplish. That is, Naylor has, in
fact, employed deconstruction as a narrative technique to uncover the
ambiguities, flaws, gaps, and contradictions in life in general, and in 1948
America in particular.

The title setting provides the ideal example of Naylor's strategy. Bailey's sits on the margin, with the real world on the front side and an
abyss (marking "infinite possibility") in the rear. In this cafe, almost anything can, and does, happen. In that void in the rear of the cafe Mariam
gives birth to her son George who offers hope and life in a place where
many have lost inspiration by accepting the impositions (labels, burdens)
placed on them. The notion of "possibility" that is engendered in that
open space (or gap) at the rear of the cafe is central to deconstructionist
doctrine. Deconstructionists do not attempt to "destroy" meaning by
highlighting ambiguities or contradictions; rather, they strive to uncover
a multiplicity of meanings, or possibilities.

Bailey himself is a key figure to this concept of deconstruction. Admitting that his name is not even Bailey, and admitting in the last chapter
that the cafe is not even his, he underscores the arbitrariness of labels.
Bailey is not the fixed symbol to identify the man, or person, he is. It is
useful only in this particular story, but in another context, he might be
called by another name. Or even more important is the fact that the
symbol is less important than the signified. That is, in this case the person
underneath the label is more important than the label. But in order to
appreciate this fact, one must be willing to get to know the person and
not be influenced, or even discouraged, by the mere label.

Bailey's wife Nadine offers another perfect study in deconstructionist
characterization. Rejecting all preconceptions of standard behavior, Nadine is one who demands that her uniqueness be accepted. As Bailey
critiques, although most important happenings are "below the surface
[also a deconstructionist tenet], other people do come up for air and
translate their feelings for the general population now and then. Nadine
doesn't bother. You figure her out or leave her alone" (19). Nadine does
not allow for a mere "surface" reading of her personality. Of course, one

could try to define her by assessing her only superficially, but one would not have an accurate appraisal of her individual personality. Early in their courtship Bailey even makes the mistake of trying to understand Nadine by evaluating her on what he considers normal behaviors. Concerned that she is not enjoying herself on one of their dates, Bailey questions her on her constant refusal to smile, only to receive the following response: "But what does that [smiling] have to do with being pleased?" (17). Completely miffed, Bailey is at a loss for words. However, Nadine has, in essence, deconstructed one aspect of acceptable human behavior. The smile could be read as a mere symbol that, in Nadine's estimation, has no bearing on her actual mood (read "signified"). And in the same way that Saussure examines arbitrariness as a result of moving from one language to another (with a different set of symbols, or signifiers), Nadine's seemingly bizarre response is also subject to the same examination. In another culture, or language, her smiling might in fact have nothing to do with being pleased.

Practically every element in this novel serves to subvert accepted ideas of reality and meaning. In this way Naylor forces readers to reassess their own personal notions of normalcy and to reclaim a pattern of learning that appreciates questions as much as it does easy answers.

The Men of Brewster Place
(1998)

In her fifth novel Naylor returns to the community she created in her first novel, *The Women of Brewster Place* (1982). In this second installment, however, the men offer their perspectives on the issues that have challenged not only their community, but also their self-perceptions and their relationships with the women in their lives. These men are more dynamic characters; they show growth and development, as the reader garners a more complete sense of their internal drives and their frustrations, as well as their aspirations and pride-filled moments of achievement. In addition to revisiting the men who appeared in *The Women of Brewster Place*, Naylor also introduces a few new characters who serve as unifying agents in the overall text. Though ostensibly set in the same time period that frames *The Women of Brewster Place* this fifth novel extends more closely to the present. In this way, Naylor expands her poetic license in order to make contemporary observations and applications.

PLOT DEVELOPMENT

As is true of *The Women of Brewster Place* (1982), *The Men of Brewster Place* is composed of short stories, each of which details the life of a particular character. The first story presents Ben, the maintenance man for Brewster Place, who not only narrates his own tale but also introduces the remaining chapters in the book. It is his voice, then, that unifies the novel. In the "Ben" chapter the reader charts Ben's journey from childhood to his present sixty-eight-year-old life, while Ben himself fleshes out key events from his past so as to present himself as a whole being and not merely a one-dimensional stereotype. Throughout his adult life, Ben has been dismissed as a useless alcoholic; however, this condition did not emerge out of nothing. Like Ben himself, his current situation has a history, one directly connected to the most troublesome, out of many, disappointments that plague his life.

Ben's life of frustration is presented not as an isolated circumstance; rather, his is a story that has shaped the lives of other black men much like him. This argument is supported when Ben details his family history, especially that of his grandfather. Raised by his Grandma and Grandpa Jones, Ben grew up hearing much about their young lives during slavery, and he watched as his grandfather developed into more of a silent and bitter man. It is much later in life before Ben discovers the cause of his grandfather's anger. When the old man was a twelve-year-old slave, he witnessed one of the most horrific tragedies that could be visited upon a child. After his ten-year-old sister is raped by the plantation overseer, the boy is sent on horseback by his mistress to enlist the aid of the doctor, once it is discovered that the young girl is in dire need of medical attention. Frantic and scared, upon arriving at the doctor's, the child rushes to the front door, only to be intercepted by a black house slave, who directs him to the back and forces him to wait incessantly in punishment for his error. By the time he and the doctor return to the plantation, his sister is dead. Now completely devastated, the future Grandpa Jones waits in vain for some acknowledgment of wrong, for some kind of accountability. When the bewildered boy cries out "No, No" at his sister's funeral, his own mother slaps him and admonishes him to be quiet and act like a man.

The lesson that his grandfather learns and the one that Ben, and other black men like him, will learn is that to be a man is to be strong and silent, to suppress weakness, a lesson consistent with a traditional definition of manhood in general. But in the case of these black men who witness various atrocities in a lifetime, such an admonition of silence seems particularly perverse. While his grandfather retreats from society and turns his anger inward (he keeps waiting for a vengeful God to strike down all things evil), Ben also develops into a kind of hermit, but he adds alcohol to the isolation.

Much of Ben's present pain stems not only from the fact that the majority society ignores, or represses, his manhood, but also from the troublesome realization that not much has changed for black manhood since the days of slavery. After leaving home at seventeen in the early 1940s upon the death of his grandmother (his grandfather having died ten years earlier), Ben works for a while cleaning spittoons in a Memphis hotel, only to be spat on daily; then, he shines shoes in a railroad depot, that is, until he meets his future wife, Elvira. Convincing Ben that her health requires fresh country air, Ben reluctantly returns to an agricultural life.

Finding themselves sharecropping on a farm owned by Mr. Clyde Haggard, Ben and Elvira attempt to eke out a living. Even years after the birth of their slightly crippled daughter (and only child), they are merely scraping by. An increasingly belligerent Elvira accuses Ben of being less than a man because he cannot spirit them away to better economic circumstances. As a result Ben becomes even more frustrated with feelings of inadequacy. And then when his now teenage daughter, who cleans house for Mr. Clyde, reports to him and Elvira that the old man has molested her, Ben feels all the more emasculated, especially when Elvira, in denial, refuses to acknowledge the validity of their daughter's accusation. Elvira even threatens to strike Ben if, either by commission (questioning Mr. Clyde directly) or omission (refusing to grin and smile when Mr. Clyde approaches), Ben challenges Mr. Clyde in any way. Ben realizes that his only alternative is to "be quiet and act like a man," instead of defending his daughter's honor and redefining manhood for himself.

After his daughter finally flees from home, stating in a note that if she has to prostitute herself to Mr. Clyde, she might as well go to Memphis where she can really make some money, Ben tries to assuage his guilt by drinking heavily. He wakes up one day to find that, even after all of his emotional and physical sacrifices, Elvira has abandoned him. Though he describes her action as being an actual favor, he is still burdened with the belief that much of his life has been a nightmare because he has been left with so few choices, and the ones offered him are ultimately self-defeating.

The next chapter, which Ben narrates entirely, introduces seventeen-year-old autistic resident Brother Jerome, gifted pianist and neighborhood celebrity who possesses only a three-year-old mind. The very short tale highlights the discovery of Jerome's talent and his meteoric rise to local fame. Born to an indifferent and self-absorbed woman, Mildred (known far and wide for her robust house parties), Jerome was almost cast aside and institutionalized before his mother realized his special skill. On the night before Jerome's impending departure, the then five-year-old is feted with a going-away party (Mildred, of course, employs any excuse to host a social).

During the festivities young Jerome, unnoticed by the partygoers, moves to the piano and begins playing expertly. Now finding herself in the midst of genius, Mildred decides not to exile Jerome; rather she exploits his talent by now charging admission to her house parties. And for the next twelve years, she makes a modest living, in addition to her blue-collar job, with the help of a young man whose presence she was once willing to forgo.

The chapter following returns to a character from *The Women of Brewster Place*. In the first novel Basil Michael abandons his mother Mattie after she uses her house as security for his bail, resulting in Mattie's losing the house and removing to Brewster Place. The chapter opens with a remorseful thirty-five-year-old Basil, three years after his sudden flight, standing at Mattie's grave site and wishing he could undo the emotional damage inflicted on his mother and apologize to her. The reader soon discovers a man quite clearly more mature than he was just a few years prior. Basil reveals that he has spent the last three years working two full-time jobs and one part-time job in an attempt to earn enough money to restore his mother to her own home. But just as he prepares to surprise her with his news and her good fortune, Basil discovers that Mattie is dead.

In an attempt to redeem himself, Basil decides that he will find some woman, make her his wife, and ultimately become the kind of loving and supportive father he never had. Quite determined in his agenda, Basil begins to date the boss's secretary, Helen, a respectable person who is pursuing her own dream of earning a graduate degree. However, soon after they begin seeing each other, Basil meets Helen's cousin Keisha, a twenty-year-old unmarried welfare recipient with two young boys. Fearful that he might not be able to father his own children, Basil decides that he should become a father figure to Jason and Eddie, quite to Helen's consternation. Ultimately, he and Helen dissolve their relationship, and Basil assumes a fatherly role in the life of the boys, deciding finally that he must marry Keisha, though he really does not love her, so that he can adopt the boys and give them a normal home life.

Two years into the marriage Basil discovers that Keisha has been unfaithful to him with her drug-addicted ex-boyfriend. Confronting her on what he considers the emotional abuse of his sons (subjecting them to a criminal), Basil soon finds himself engrossed in a bitter argument with Keisha, one that ends with his slapping her, an act that he immediately regrets. Finding that he cannot reason with Keisha, Basil, in what is merely a scare tactic, threatens to take the boys and leave. A few days later Basil finds himself confronting a bench warrant for his arrest. Keisha has reported to the police that Basil is a five-year fugitive, a circumstance about which she cared nothing when Basil admitted it to her prior to their marriage (then, of course, he was her new cash cow). Now Basil must explain to young Eddie and Jason, both of whom adore their stepfather but both of whom are still sensitive to abandonment, why he must leave them. By the time Basil returns a few years later, the boys have become hardened and distant. Yet Basil is determined to win their respect and trust once again.

While Basil is left to fight for the love of his sons, in the next chapter Eugene Turner is left to fight for his identity. In *The Women of Brewster Place* Eugene is presented as the cowardly husband who intends to abandon his wife and daughter, and while in the throes of an argument with wife Ciel about his impending departure, Eugene (along with Ciel) endures the most painful moment of his life, the accidental electrocution of two-year-old daughter Serena. In this self-narrated chapter, Eugene presents a comprehensive portrait of himself in an attempt to explain his complex personality.

Eugene's problem is not that he feels financially strapped; it is not even that he has fallen out of love with Ciel. Eugene has simply begun to awaken to his own homosexual urges. Instead of confronting these desires, however, he creates tension and fuels arguments with Ciel, in the hope that she will initiate a permanent separation so that he will not have to make a definite decision. But as the months pass, Eugene finds that he can no longer repress his true feelings. Braving new experiences, Eugene ventures out to gay clubs, ironically with the help of his very macho boss Bruce, reluctantly finding himself more and more comfortable in the presence of these men. Then after he finally experiences physical contact with a man, and feels a sense of wholeness he has never known before, Eugene is terminated at work. Now, with the growing sense of his real sexual identity yet with the added burden of having to secure a new job to support a lifestyle to which he is no longer emotionally committed, Eugene feels cornered, and his only resolution is escape, no matter the cost.

Once again, Eugene tries to initiate an argument with Ciel, but she remains calm in an elusive attempt to reason with Eugene. Finally, wanting desperately to salvage her marriage, Ciel resorts to the grievous decision to abort her second child. Feeling guilty, Eugene stays for another six months. Then, no longer capable of living the lie and overwhelmed with unrelenting guilt, Eugene decides to leave. While he and Ciel are arguing about his decision, the toddling Serena, trying to entertain herself by chasing a roach, inserts a fork into an electrical socket and is killed instantly. While Ciel is unconsolable during the ensuing days and weeks following Serena's death, Eugene becomes practically catatonic. Concluding ultimately that he can no longer bear the emotional pain, he finds a way to inflict physical pain on himself. The chapter ends with Eugene visiting the apartment of Chino, a gender-neutral sadomasochist whom he met in a club, and willingly enduring the repeated whipping that Chino grudgingly inflicts on a supplicant Eugene.

Eugene seeks redemption, but in the following chapter the Reverend Moreland T. Woods desires exaltation. Believing unabashedly that he is a savior, Reverend Woods thinks he deserves unequivocal acknowledgment of his self-defined stature. Unsatisfied with the fact that he has amassed a congregation numbering in the hundreds, he wants to increase those numbers exponentially and perhaps even tap the resources of broadcast evangelism. These desires/efforts are grounded not so much in an altruistic need to minister to the less fortunate, but rather in an obsessive impulse to propel himself to superstardom and later transform himself into a politician.

The Reverend's only obstacle is an officers board whose members refuse to authorize the construction of a new church. Woods, with designs ultimately on the mayor's office, believes that with a larger building he could increase the number of congregants and solidify his political might in the community. The minister thinks that if only Deacon Bennett, his all-time nemesis, were to support his efforts, the other deacons would follow suit.

Following a discordant meeting with the officers board and finding himself without any alternative, Woods threatens to take the matter before the entire congregation for a referendum, as allowed by the church bylaws, while Bennett and the others urge him not to proceed, lest he suffer embarrassment and bring unnecessary turmoil to the church family. Completely unflappable, Woods petitions the membership for a referendum, to be held two months away. In the interim, both factions lobby members for support, with Bennett spreading rumors that building a new church will deplete all funds and with Woods preaching fiery sermons about the hardships borne when one struggles to save an ungrateful people.

Suddenly one day an unmarried and pregnant young woman, Sister Louise, visits Woods in his office to seek solace about her condition, revealing as well that she is unsure about the paternity of her child, though one possibility is, in fact, one of the deacons. Woods realizes that at the very least, his prayers have been answered. On an appointed Sunday, the Reverend preaches an impassioned sermon about sin and redemption, after which he asks that the anonymous deacon reveal himself and bravely shoulder a portion of Sister Louise's shame. Knowing that no one will emerge and knowing that as a result of such refusal the membership will begin to scorn the entire officers board, Woods, now in full dramatic form, intensifies his plea to the errant father who, of course, never surfaces. Now completely miffed with the unknown villain, the congregation decides to support the Reverend's efforts in erecting a new building.

The Moreland T. Woods' story concerns church politics, but the next chapter addresses street politics, or gang warfare. This chapter finds C. C. Baker, a local drug runner, under question by two detectives regarding a recent murder. Throughout, C. C. continues to deny that he knows any of the drug lords and gang leaders about whom he is asked. And he especially denies knowledge of the circumstances of the murder, the victim of which happens to be his stepbrother. The entire chapter consists of dialogue between the two detectives, black males themselves, and C. C.

Even after they present to C. C. their theory of what occurred, he demurs. According to the detectives, C. C. works for one of the most notorious drug dealers in the area, one Beetle Royal, while C. C.'s stepbrother Hakim worked for rival dealer Tito. The detectives hypothesize that as a test of loyalty Royal ordered C. C. to assassinate Hakim. Nevertheless, C. C. insists that he is not only innocent of such a crime but also ignorant of all circumstances and persons therein related to it.

Interspersed in this chapter are flashback sections that detail C. C.'s emergence as one of Royal's lackeys and the gradual development of misplaced pride when C. C. can provide his family with the accouterments that elude his father. C. C. becomes the man of the house as his own father sinks further and further into an invisible nothingness. Enjoying his newfound status in a family that refuses even to question the source of his funds, C. C. becomes even more hardened in his determination to "succeed" in the world of the street. Thus, when Royal issues his challenge, or ultimatum, to the man-child, C. C. believes he has no alternative but to murder Hakim. And now, even though the detectives are firmly convinced that C. C. is the culprit, C. C. still denies involvement, opting instead to uphold the rules of his gang world, a world where he, in a misguided and woefully distorted way, feels worthy and relevant.

While the C. C. Baker chapter presents the worst elements on the street, the Clifford Montgomery Jackson (or Abshu) chapter represents the best. Head of the neighborhood community center, Abshu is quite committed to improving the lives of otherwise ignored and/or abused children. His current dilemma concerns not children, however, but rather a key member of the city council, none other than Rev. Moreland T. Woods. In the opening scene to this chapter Abshu, perturbed that Woods has betrayed the very community that elected him to office by voting for the demolition of Brewster Place, is plotting the metaphoric murder of Woods. Having grown up in a foster home isolated from his siblings, Abshu is particularly sensitive to issues of abandonment and feelings of vulnerability. Fearing that many of the current residents of Brewster may find themselves homeless, Abshu thinks that Woods' political maneuver is at the very least despicable, if not completely obscene.

Having exhausted all of his options for encouraging Woods to reconsider his vote, Abshu is desperate to devise a plan that will punish the Reverend. On one occasion when Abshu and his streetwise attorney friend B. B. Rey are discussing this problem, the two men decide upon a course of action. On the day of the next scheduled meeting of the city council, B. B. Rey amasses a crowd of fifty women, all actresses, who begin to picket outside council chambers and to chant: "Moreland, Moreland / Where's your shame? / You left and didn't give / My baby a name" (150). Seizing an opportunity to exploit one of Woods' weaknesses (women), B. B. Rey and Abshu simply retreat and observe the full impact of the rally. Because the women cause such an uproar the council is forced to adjourn for the day, and ultimately the council asks for Woods' resignation. Opting not to fight, lest one of the women is telling the truth, Woods honors the request and relinquishes his seat. Though Abshu feels a slight sense of accomplishment, he still questions this strategy, especially given the fact that Woods is replaced on the council with a white conservative. While it is true that Woods felt no remorse for betraying his own community, Abshu does feel a pang of guilt for his part in Woods' defeat.

The final chapter is set in the barbershop, the neighborhood haven for men. Here, the black male clientele, "armchair—or barber chair politician[s]" (158), discuss politics, namely the tension between black men and white men: "The white man carries all the guilt for messing up the world; the black man gets all the blame" (158). They also discuss women, who they think are beyond comprehension. It is in the barbershop that these men can offer their opinions and vent their frustrations without censorship or ridicule. Though they may feel burdened in their domestic space or demeaned outside their own community, they know that within the domain of the barbershop they rule unobtrusively.

Serving as the climactic ending to the novel, the barbershop scene culminates in a horrific moment that challenges the equilibrium sedulously maintained in this black male sanctuary. One of the frequent customers is the homeless Greasy. Though he was once a thriving airline employee with his own home and family, the crack-addicted Greasy now finds himself wandering mindlessly through the streets of Brewster Place. Barbershop owner Max, whose two-chair establishment caters to all the men in the neighborhood, always welcomes Greasy in and gives him a free cut. Because Greasy's behavior can be volatile, Max always ushers Greasy immediately to a chair so that Greasy can leave as quickly as possible. All other patrons understand this tactic and support Max in his effort, even though some of them may be inconvenienced in the effort.

On this one occasion Greasy enters the business and soon begins his typical tirade, "I'm a man. I'm a man" (165), whereupon he also seizes hold of Max's employee Henry and threatens to stab him. Max and the waiting customers attempt to calm Greasy down, a struggle that takes some time. Suddenly, though, Greasy releases Henry, and in that same instant, Greasy slits his own throat and sends blood gushing all over the shop. The chapter ends with the men speculating on what they might have done to prevent Greasy's suicide and with their having to reconcile the demise of Brewster Place, which, with the assistance of Moreland Woods, has been slated for demolishment along with Max's barbershop.

The last section of the novel, a brief epilogue, witnesses a forlorn Abshu walking through the now ghostlike neighborhood of Brewster Place. He wonders if he could have done anything more to save this place he has called home. Though Abshu is saddened by the death of Brewster, he is determined to believe that all of his efforts were not futile, that in fact this most recent struggle was mere practice for him to wage more battles in the future.

CHARACTER DEVELOPMENT

As stated earlier, the main characters in this novel reappear from *The Women of Brewster Place* in order to explain more fully their often confusing behaviors in that first novel and to present themselves as evolving personalities. Serving as philosopher/observer, Ben's development is presented in two ways. First, his insights into the struggles of the other men reveal an intellectual profundity that one might stereotypically consider unusual for someone like Ben. Second, Ben's present outlook on life, in short his personality, is made more intelligible once one gains a comprehensive understanding of his past. Ben's most pronounced insight about the other men is presented early in the novel, and it serves to characterize not only the social reality of these other men, but also Ben's skill in recognizing that reality. Ben suggests that any man, whether he lives on Park Avenue or the south side of Chicago, can feel worthless if he is denied affirmation and support. Ben understands that a man's circumstances are less important than his attitude and level of hope and promise about those circumstances. A wealthy Park Avenue man can be just as forlorn as a poor man in Chicago's South Side if his self-esteem is diminished. It is the "inside," the spiritual and emotional grounding, of a man that affects him most. When one considers all that Ben has endured throughout his life—growing up with an embittered grandfather, being thrust into the world to survive at an early age, suffering through a loveless marriage, and finding himself unable to protect his only child—and when one observes Ben's rather philosophical response, one finds a man who has learned from his experiences.

When Ben is presented in *The Women of Brewster Place*, the reader is given a suitable composite of a man whose present demoralized state is linked to his feelings of inadequacy about his role as father and protector. The kindness he extends to Lorraine in that novel, the reader comes to understand, is his attempt to redeem himself for failing his daughter. However, in *The Men of Brewster Place*, Naylor expands the scope of Ben's background as a means of highlighting the fact that Ben's limitations are not just personal; rather they are linked to very real social circumstances. In this way, Ben's present alcoholism is not just the manifestation of an empty shell of a man. It serves, instead, as an indication of strong manhood, only in a frustrated state. When Naylor links Ben's inability to protect his daughter to his Grandpa Jones's feelings of weakness and cowardice because as a boy he could not protect his sister, she is reminding the reader that just as it would be unfair to criticize a boy for his inability to perform a "manly," or brave feat, it is unfair to judge a man like Ben who has been rendered impotent (or "boylike") by societal encumbrances. In short, the reader must assess Ben's life comprehensively in order to appreciate its complexity.

Basil's development is the result of internal changes. Having engaged in much soul-searching and introspection, Basil takes full responsibility for ruining his mother's life. In *The Women of Brewster Place* Basil is depicted as a spoiled, selfish brat, even as a thirty-year-old. That his mother even had to live in Brewster Place was the result of Basil's self-centered behavior. Now, however, Basil has transformed himself from being a taker to being a giver, a change highlighted when Basil offers a prayer of thanks for all that his mother sacrificed. That Basil expresses gratitude and thanks is indicative of personal growth. In addition, however, when he thanks her for not sapping all of her funds on his behalf, he reveals the fact that he fully understands that she had already expended more than enough energy and money on his behalf. The latter comment suggests that Basil would like to reverse all of the actions that his mother made on his behalf; in short, he wishes he could retract the selfish requests and demands he exacted on his mother's good nature. Basil's development, too, is the result of his now shouldering the guilt that he made his mother feel in *The Women of Brewster Place* when she initially suggested that he stay in jail until his trial. Some of the pain he caused her he is now feeling and bravely enduring.

Bearing pain courageously is also the stamp of Eugene's growth. When introduced in *The Women of Brewster Place*, Eugene, like Basil, was presented as callous and mean-spirited, belittling his wife for sport. In *The Men of Brewster Place*, however, Eugene offers an extended apology to Ciel as he attempts to explain his past behavior. By giving voice to his struggle, Eugene exposes his vulnerabilities, and in so doing he strengthens his resolve to be a better man. He realizes now that his former hardened macho image was merely an attempt to hide his insecurities. When donning these masks, Eugene became an empty shell, lacking the very strength he wished to project. Now that he has divested himself of these masks Eugene has positioned himself for further growth. And though his method for effecting this growth is rather unorthodox—enduring the sadistic physical abuse inflicted by Chino—at the very least Eugene is willing to share the pain that he now knows Ciel must have felt emotionally during the marriage and certainly upon Serena's death.

Minor characters include Elvira, Mildred, Keisha, Mr. Clyde, Deacon

Bennett, and B. B. Rey. The three women are significant in balancing the portraits of the men, as they refute the misguided notion that only men behave insensitively. The women's actions are particularly despicable because they exploit not only the men in their lives, but also the children. In addition to emasculating husband Ben, whether criticizing him for not fathering more children or belittling him for their living conditions, Elvira also abuses her daughter when she refuses to acknowledge the girl's accusations about being molested. She forces the child to leave home, and then once she has all but destroyed what little esteem Ben had, Elvira abandons him. Mildred and Keisha also demean the men and/or children in their lives. Mildred initially intends to institutionalize (abandon) son Jerome, but once she discovers that the autistic child is talented (and may benefit her), she decides to keep him, not out of love or concern, but out of greed and selfishness. Keisha harms both Basil and her two sons when she reports Basil to the authorities. Instead of admitting her own faults in a mature fashion, she projects them onto Basil, initiates his arrest, and leaves her sons without a male role model. With these women characters Naylor shows how women are just as responsible as men for domestic tensions. Mr. Clyde represents the white patriarchal institutions that all the black characters, men and women, must confront at some time. Though he functions in Ben's former life, his presence is still felt in the contemporary moment as a means of acknowledging the constant, though sometimes subtle, impact of white male authority.

While all of the aforementioned characters represent, in some way, the opposition that confronts black men, the other two minor characters reinforce positive black male response to the various oppositions. As leader in his church community, Deacon Bennett desires to improve the condition of that community by encouraging the church to expand its outreach to economic projects. Understanding that contemporary civil rights initiatives must include an economic component, Bennett is poised to rally the church around such efforts. Instead of bemoaning his ineffectiveness in the "white" world, Bennett assumes leadership in the "black" world where he can have an impact. B. B. Rey, like Deacon Bennett, possesses both intellectual depth and practical "streetwise" knowledge. In his effort to remove Reverend Woods from the city council, B. B. Rey reveals his understanding that one must sometimes employ unorthodox methods to achieve the greater good. And when one considers the fact that the B. B. Reys and Deacon Bennetts must combat not only the Mr. Clydes of the world, but also the Elviras, Mildreds, and Keishas, one better understands why black manhood might adopt a position of "moral flexibility" merely to survive.

THEMATIC ISSUES

The dominant theme in this novel is presented in the question, "What defines black manhood?" Each of the main characters finds himself in a search for identity in a world that, according to Ralph Ellison's *Invisible Man*, would rather not see him at all. Given the black man's inherent struggle, then, with the majority population, his very existence as a survivor is an affront to the tenets of white supremacy. As a consequence, the black man has been forced to adopt the posture of silence and to mask feelings of frustration and anger lest such expressions render dangerous repercussions. As Ben states, in his recollections about his silent and stern grandfather, black men were told that the only way to be a man was to suffer quietly. While one may suggest that men in general have been indoctrinated to suffer in silence and to exhibit strength by denying pain, such a burden for the black man is particularly taxing, because even if the white man were to complain about his pain, all he might suffer would be ridicule (the white man with complete power would not suffer even this). But if the black man were to express his pain (obviously in opposition to the white man who is inflicting the pain), he would be summarily abused, if not lynched.

It is this reality that confronts some of the characters. Consequently, they suppress all feelings that might be construed as signs of weakness. The ironic result of this posture, however, is that the resultant silence is then defined as a hardened machismo that almost obliterates even a semblance of humanity. In short, the black man is caught in a no-win situation. The coping strategies they choose, especially when viewed in the absence of a knowledge of the social or historical context that forces the strategies, become emblems of antisocial, or disturbed, behavior. For example, when Ben discovers that he is powerless to protect his daughter from Mr. Clyde's molestation, he resorts to alcohol, thinking that if he numbs himself, he can endure the pain that such vulnerability causes. Some might view this strategy as self-defeatist, as weak; however, Ben explains the ultimate motivation here, and his paradoxical statement serves to highlight the seeming contradiction between defining the ploy as an act of tragedy or an act of courage: "So I settled on killing myself—

slowly with booze—and on God understanding that I'm fighting for my manhood" (28). Certainly, one opinion might be that Ben is a hopeless alcoholic who exhibits antisocial behavior; thus his is a tragic downfall. However, when Ben states that he is fighting to salvage his manhood, one realizes that his drinking is actually an act of courage, for he still thinks he has a manhood worth saving.

Like Ben, the other men in the novel also confront this almost impossible struggle with defining manhood. Basil, for example, tries to achieve manhood first by acknowledging his past mistakes (jumping bail and abandoning his mother, cowardly acts that result in her losing her house) and then by trying to redeem himself by bettering the lives of a single mother and her sons and, in turn, contributing positively to society. Yet Basil's circumstances reveal the paradoxical relationship between black men and the justice system. Though Basil's attorney assures him (in *The Women of Brewster Place*) that he will be exonerated, as the day of the trial draws nearer, Basil becomes more and more paranoid about his plight. Even though he knows that the man he is accused of murdering in a barroom brawl simply struck his head on the bar when Basil pushed him away in self-defense, Basil still fears that he will be found guilty of murder and imprisoned. Sensitive to the historical reality of the black man's treatment by the legal system and consequently distrusting that system, he flees. And now five years later, as a married man with his two adopted sons, Basil tries to prove that he is no longer that scared young man; rather he is now an independent person in charge of his own destiny. Unfortunately, the newfound growth is short-lived. Basil's arrest, at the hands of his wife, provides the cosmic irony that so often seems to plague the lives of the black men in the novel. Basil is arrested for involuntary manslaughter, not for jumping bail. And though he has tried, over these few years, to atone for the pain he inflicted on his mother, his very act of atonement (providing for two young boys) is hampered when he is incarcerated (the same punishment he feared years ago though he was assured he would be spared). At every turn, it would seem, Basil's attempts at manhood are thwarted. To exacerbate matters, his sudden departure from Eddie and Jason has a detrimental effect. By the time Basil satisfies his six-year sentence, Jason, now fifteen, has served time in juvenile detention, and Eddie, now thirteen, has begun to manifest antisocial behavior. The novel seems to suggest, in this depiction, that black manhood is forever doomed to failure, that all societal elements collude to undermine its efforts to thrive. Nevertheless, Basil is determined to restore humanity to these boys, if he must spend the remainder of his life doing so, forever fighting to combat the social odds.

While Basil's battle is an external one with society, Eugene's is an internal struggle between his perception of manhood and the reality of his own emotional/sexual impulses. In the past Eugene accepted the notion that only a heterosexual existence defined manhood, masculinity, or manliness. And if one harbors homoerotic feelings, he risks losing his gender identity. Consequently, Eugene tries desperately to sustain his marital relationship. He keeps returning because he needs his role as husband and father to define him as a true man. Without these titles, he feels inadequate. The irony in Eugene's circumstances is that after he returns and attempts a semblance of familial commitment, he feels even more inadequate, and this inadequacy is twofold: (1) he is not emotionally bound to this heterosexual existence; and (2) if he were, because of his economic limitations, Eugene cannot provide his wife and daughter with even a minimal standard of living. Like both Ben and Basil, Eugene suffers paradoxically. Eugene needs Ciel and Serena in order to feel like a man, yet because he does not have the economic power of his white counterparts, he feels less than a man when he is with them. Eugene's psychological dilemma is personified in the form of Chino, the would-be transgendered barfly Eugene encounters. Neither quite male nor quite female (having stopped the process of being transformed from a man to a woman), Chino is left suspended in a gender warp. Like Eugene, Chino was once beholden to society's definition of who he should be, but now realizing that society, in its capricious appraisal of humanity, will forever confuse and thwart individual identity no matter how obedient that individual identity is, Chino rejects societal intrusion and defines himself. Fully understanding the plight of the misunderstood, Chino cautions Eugene that he should divorce Ciel, lest he make her life even more miserable. Yet Eugene ignores the advice, and when he does not end the relationship, he ends up losing his daughter. Eugene learns too late that his manhood is not contingent on his accepting external definitions of who he is or should be. Now that he is no longer a husband or father, he will have to claim manhood in some other way, one consistent with his individual self.

Just as Eugene is ill-equipped to create a concept of manhood that benefits him, C. C. Baker cannot imagine any notion of manhood unsanctioned by society. For C. C. the very accouterments that society insists a true man possess must be enhanced and embellished, almost to the level of obsession. In short, C. C. hungers for money, power, and respect. And if acquiring these "tokens" of manhood requires illegal activities, then he will accept the challenge. It is quite clear that C. C. has a distorted view of manhood, yet he has simply embraced the definition meted out in the popular culture. Unfortunately, when one requires external objects (money, power, and in the case of C. C., a gun) to define oneself, once those objects are lost or seized, one's manhood is lost as well. So even though someone like C. C. feels himself powerful because of his acquisitions, he is, in fact, made weaker with every "necessary" acquisition. Once he has no power to lord over anyone else, once he has no one to make feel inferior, then he is lost and empty.

C. C.'s attitude about respect is also distorted. Not understanding that one earns, or commands, respect, he harbors the misguided notion that one can "demand" respect, when in fact one is only "demanding" fear. When C. C. reveals that he has lost respect for his father because his father cannot provide the luxuries that C. C. provides with his ill-gotten gain and because his father blindly accepts C. C.'s gifts without question, C. C. fails to understand that his father's sense of manhood is not necessarily linked to the empty tokens C. C. provides or to an acknowledgment of C. C.'s fortune. Perhaps his father's reticence is a move to allow his family some material pleasure without intruding upon C. C.'s turf. C. C.'s perverted sense of manhood is made even clearer when in the final moment of the chapter he murders his stepbrother Hakim and then runs away, grateful for "The courage to be a man" (129).

While C. C. maintains the most warped view of manhood, Abshu provides the most wholesome perspective. A compassionate warrior, Abshu fights for the betterment of society in general and of Brewster Place in particular, providing a voice for the needy and disenfranchised. Abshu is a strong man because he understands how one should define himself as a man: "Do whatever job makes you happy, regardless of the cost; and fill your home with love" (140). He embraces very simple philosophical concepts. Instead of feverishly struggling to acquire as many trinkets as he can, Abshu advocates pursuing a job that provides emotional and spiritual fulfillment. In short, the true man looks within himself for definition rather than without, and once he has a stable emotional foundation, he can withstand the various external pressures.

In addition, Abshu practices one important tenet of black manhood, first advocated by Frederick Douglass in his original narrative: engaging in physical retaliation only as a last resort. Instead of fighting, one should use his wits to best his opponent. At one point in the "Abshu" chapter, one of Abshu's pupils finds himself and his friends being bullied by some slightly older boys. In an effort to teach the young boys how to use their intellect, Abshu teaches them to curse like Shakespearean characters do. Instead of using profanity, the utterance of which might result in violence, the boys learn to make pronouncements such as "you drone," "you cur," or "you base wretch." Completely miffed by such strange language, the older boys ultimately retreat. Successes like these not only provide the young boys with the confidence to confront future challenges but also encourage Abshu that his often unheralded actions are relevant and effective.

Abshu's unyielding commitment to these young boys and their futures provides the basis for his disenchantment with Moreland Woods. Because Abshu tries to honor his own responsibilities, he expects the same from other so-called men, especially those who have assumed a leadership role with the help of the community. When Woods betrays Brewster Place by advocating its demolition, Abshu practically comes unhinged at the prospect that Woods would be allowed to maintain his seat on the city council. Abshu's loyalty to his friends and neighbors completely outweighs any allegiance he might have felt to the lone black member of the council. In this case, challenging and ultimately defeating a black man (one whose interests are not consistent with those of the black community) strengthens Abshu's self-respect and thus his manhood.

Abshu's sense of brotherhood and communion with others in the community is echoed in the final chapter, set in the barbershop. This scene serves as a wake-up call to black men to honor and respect each other; in so doing, they honor and respect themselves. Even though Greasy seems alienated from the rest of the community, he is still one of them. Unlike C. C., who wreaks havoc on the lives of others, Greasy hurts only himself (his wife and children have long since stopped depending on him). Yet when Greasy commits suicide, all of the men in the shop are affected by the tragedy. In the final analysis, they feel as though they have failed Greasy because they lost sight of the humanity that is common to all.

As a collective body, the barbershop clients did not adopt a wholesome notion of manhood in regard to Greasy. Instead they, ironically, adopted the model of the oppressor. They made themselves feel better about themselves by distancing themselves from Greasy's plight. Their sense of self, then, was dependent on the ostensible inferiority of another (the oppressor-oppressed model). As black men trying to function in a racist world, they should have been sensitive to this degrading tool. They realize this, of course, too late, as far as Greasy is concerned.

This thematic lesson in black manhood involves more than just a unifying bond for men. It also recognizes the importance of embracing womanhood in tandem with manhood. Rejecting the oppressive model that treats women as inferior beings, emergent and progressive black manhood defines as one of its primary roles the affirmation of women. Though this novel attends primarily to the men, the narrative voice reminds the reader that women figure prominently in the lives of these men. According to Ben, "I don't know a man who would be anywhere without a woman. And don't know a woman who'd be anywhere without a man. It's how God did it; and we sure can't undo it" (7). After all, concludes Ben, "there was always a Her in his story" (8).

HISTORICAL CONTEXT

Since the antebellum period African-American manhood has been an important issue in the struggle for black autonomy and equality. From the transformative moment in his *Narrative of the Life of Frederick Douglass, An American Slave* (1845), when Douglass announces that he will no longer participate in his own subjugation at the hands of overseer Mr. Covey, African-American manhood has unfolded as the premier metaphor for African-American agency. In short, if African-American males could gain acknowledgment of their strength, their intellect, and their devotion and loyalty to their families, then other members of their race would achieve recognition of their humanity. Attaining manhood also entailed defying black stereotypes. From slavery to the present day, enduring and resilient black manhood has served as the mechanism by which black enfranchisement and freedom are measured. (See Literary Heritage chapter.)

It is this past to which Naylor is responding in *The Men of Brewster Place*. While the specific function of the men in this novel is to account for decisions/mistakes they made in *The Women of Brewster Place*, Naylor also uses them to establish a historical and social context. The novel is set firmly in the present, but Naylor still relies on the past (particularly in the case of Ben's story) to offer an initial basis for understanding these men. Moreover, Naylor relies on the genre of music to augment the aesthetic context and to chart the historical development of black manhood.

Of the new characters introduced in this novel, Brother Jerome emerges quite early as an important figure. With his inexplicable talent, Brother Jerome effortlessly plays the piano as he gives musical voice, in the form of blues, to the plight of black men. When Ben stresses that "the blues ain't nothing but a good man crying for help" (162), he concisely explains Jerome's role in the novel.

By playing the blues (echoing black man's pain), Jerome is performing several feats. First, he is acknowledging the humanity of the men who share the pain; second, he is linking the experiences of the men and thus offering them camaraderie; third, he is exemplifying one of the coping mechanisms black men use (creativity); and fourth, he is providing yet another means of reviewing the history of the black man in America. This blues music is directly linked to the Negro spirituals that originated in the cotton fields in the antebellum period. Those spirituals, while looking to the future for hope, were a means of coping with what seemed an impossible circumstance. By invoking the blues, Naylor clearly bows to the past while also anticipating the future. Considering the black man and his blues, Ben ponders, "Can you call it any man's blues? I don't know, but you can definitely call it the black man's blues. There's something about us and pain that keeps spinning out there in the universe to return again and again" (161). The pain that is connected to the blues is, ironically, the black man's link to his past, and if it "return[s] again and again," it will link him to his future.

Yet the black man continues to survive, just as he does at the end of the novel, and to face the challenges that lie ahead. Relying on his former invincibility, he simply plods along to eke out an existence and to effect social change whenever possible.

NARRATIVE STRUCTURE

Like *The Women of Brewster Place*, its companion novel, *The Men of Brewster Place*, is composed of short stories that provide the chapter divisions. Each story depicts the life struggle of a different man, most of whom appeared in the first novel. The only character who is afforded his own chapter yet who was not presented in *The Women of Brewster Place* is Brother Jerome, a teenage musical prodigy. With the other characters, the reader is starting ostensibly *in medias res* (or, in the middle of things), though Naylor does provide enough background detail to satisfy any lingering questions.

The novel does not employ an obvious linear movement, but there is a discernible seasonal progression. Starting in the winter, the novel, excluding the prologue and epilogue, charts a course through spring and summer, and then ends in the fall (the epilogue ends in summer), but not necessarily during a single calendar year. And because some of the individual chapters make references to past events, the time line, such as it is, is quite flexible. From a thematic standpoint, this structure is consistent with Naylor's previous novels in which she rejects fixed boundaries in an effort to register their arbitrary nature. Likewise, in *The Men of Brewster Place* the fluid nature of the narrative structure reinforces her desire not to impose any preconceived identities on the characters. Having no particular day, or no particular year, with which to "fix" the text, the reader is left with only the textual (chapter) details from which to make assessments.

There is no apparent plot connection among the various chapters (other connecting threads are evident however; see Narrative Technique section), with the exception of the "Moreland T. Woods" and "Abshu" chapters. Enjoying a meteoric rise to political fame in his own chapter, Woods is foiled in the Abshu story. All other characters are restricted to their individual chapters.

While *The Women of Brewster Place* spans the thirty-year period from the 1940s to the 1970s, *The Men of Brewster Place* spans from Ben's youth in the 1940s to his sixty-eighth year in the 1990s (and also engages in a flashback to the antebellum period). In addition to the eight "character" chapters (including the final barbershop chapter, which serves as a kind of chorus chapter), there is a prologue entitled "Dusk" and an epilogue entitled "Dawn." The prologue provides a brief history of Brewster Place, recalling the days when European immigrants resided in the neighborhood and then charting the emergence of its present-day black population. The epilogue, while detailing Brewster's demise, also offers hope, as evidenced in its title, "Dawn."

NARRATIVE TECHNIQUE

As stated above there is no apparent plot connection among the chapters. The dominant connecting thread is the narrator, Ben. Taking poetic license, as stated in an author's note that precedes the novel proper, Naylor resurrects Ben, who died at the end of *The Women of Brewster*

Place. Though he should not be considered a spirit (after all, his lifeline in *The Men of Brewster Place*—he states he has lived sixty-eight years—alerts the reader that *The Men of Brewster Place* extends into the 1990s, twenty years beyond the scope of *The Women of Brewster Place*), Ben does possess omniscient powers. With the exception of the "Basil" and "Eugene" chapters, which are narrated from the first-person perspective of the title characters (though Ben does introduce these chapters as well), all chapters are narrated by Ben. It is Ben's job, as philosopher/observer, to assess the circumstances affecting each man and then render an interpretive analysis. He refuses to intrude directly on the lives of these men (he never "appears" in their stories), but he still observes from afar, clearly positioning himself as resident expert on all matters pertaining to black men. As the more sensitive male presence in *The Women of Brewster Place*, Ben offers a stabilizing influence on the otherwise volatile gender conflicts in both novels. Since *The Men of Brewster Place* focuses primarily on the issue of black manhood, it risks ignoring the influence that women have had on that very phenomenon; however, Ben's voice reminds the reader that without the women, the men would be less than they are. In this way, then, *The Men of Brewster Place*, in tandem with *The Women of Brewster Place*, renders a more comprehensive and more balanced appraisal of black life. In addition, by designing the novel within Ben's mental ruminations, Naylor reinforces one of the dominant issues presented in the work and one, of course, that Ben introduces: the fact that all men "live *inside*" (Naylor's emphasis; 7), and even though they "cry as much as women . . . most just cry inside" (163). This is a novel that strives to penetrate the seemingly impenetrable emotional barrier that men erect and to plumb the depths of that "inside" space to recover a lost, or at least repressed, humanity. Mirroring that journey inward, or that interior space, is a narrative set in Ben's interior space (that repository of thoughts, feelings, frustrations, and aspirations). Ben is quite clear in his desire to unearth and expose those hidden pains and frustrations that plague his black male peers. Again, it is only via such investigation that black male behavior is understood. One's unwillingness to appreciate the depths of such pain simply furthers the pain, a mistake to be highlighted in the final "Barbershop" chapter.

In addition to Ben, the other unifying narrative thread is Brother Jerome and his music. Throughout the novel, Ben references Brother Jerome's blues. These musical creations give voice to the experiences of the men in the novel. The common bond among these men is persistent and sustained emotional pain. Brother Jerome's expressions provide the background for the men's lives and offer some comfort in their acknowledgment of the pain.

It stands to reason that the autistic Brother Jerome would sympathize, on some level if not consciously, with the plight of the other black men. By giving their pain expression, Brother Jerome is also acknowledging the value of their lives. Brother Jerome's presence in the novel provides a constant reminder that every life has value. Even though some might want to ignore, or even confine, someone like Jerome, he still has value, just like the men whose painful lives he embraces in his music.

A POSTCOLONIAL READING

Postcolonial criticism examines a work using the oppressor-oppressed model, whereby a colonizing group encroaches upon the physical and cultural space of another group, the colonized, and forces the latter group to adopt the value system, language, cultural practices, and sensibilities of the colonizer. The postcolonial theorist, however, is concerned with the oppressed group's rejection of previous subjugation and the restoration of its own agency and purpose, hence *post*colonial. These critics focus on issues of critical difference in literary works. Instead of ignoring the tensions these differences may create, the postcolonialist will analyze such tensions in order to learn more about each cultural position. Concerning matters of imperialism, this process often involves initiating discussions on difference that have often remained unvoiced.

For example, one might read an American novel that chronicles British colonists' gradual expansion across North America from the seventeenth century on, as it also celebrates the promise, hope, and reward of America's growth. The postcolonial critic would challenge the omission of key concerns, like the widespread genocide of Native American communities. Or the critic might question the assumption that British culture is somehow superior to others and is thus justified in "civilizing" (taking control over and ultimately suppressing) other cultures.

The postcolonial critic is concerned not just with distinct cultural spaces/positions but with hybridity, that is, the circumstance whereby individuals or groups belong to more than one culture. Perhaps most importantly, the postcolonialist deliberately acknowledges the "other" (oppressed, colonized) as a source of energy, that is, as an agent of change, and not merely as an object, especially when the "other" awakens to his or her oppressed condition.

Granted, the African-American experience differs slightly from the typical colonial experience, as the African was removed from his land and then placed in a foreign environment. Nevertheless, many of the phenomena felt in the colonizing moment impacted African life in America: forced abandonment of language, cultural suppression, severance of family bonds, etc. And like the typical colonized group, African Americans must decide at some juncture to "decolonize" themselves and try to recapture a positive sense of themselves. While a standard ploy in the decolonizing effort might be to regain land holdings and government rule, for the African American, who is no longer a part of the former physical landscape, this effort involves reclaiming his own mind and securing equity in a political and economic system that was innately designed to suppress him.

Naylor addresses both of these concerns in *The Men of Brewster Place.* To decolonize their minds, black men must first see themselves not as inferior objects, but instead as agents in their own lives who can initiate change rather than function in a passive way and merely accept dependence and defeat as normal. In order to achieve this mental leap, however, they must reassess the criteria for manhood and reject elusive standards that do not, and probably never will, apply to them. When black men compete with the white male model of success—wealth, political clout, material tokens—they find themselves feeling frustrated and inadequate, a normal reaction though to a system that has made white male success possible because it has been achieved at the expense of black labor. In short, white men are rich because black men are poor. If, then, the black man is not going to enjoy the same benefits as do white men, then he must seek different benefits. And he must rebuke white male notions of success.

Naylor analyzes this issue most decisively in the "Moreland T. Woods" and "Abshu" chapters. Woods is presented as a colonized egomaniac whose only goal is to exalt himself. He desires a larger church only because he thinks such tangible evidence of his achievement will catapult him to local political power. However, his nemesis, Deacon Bennett, free of colonizing impulses, has different goals. Because Bennett believes that "no matter what their jobs were in the outside community, or even if they had no present work, once inside the church these men became somebody, at the least, a child of God" and that "the church could be a place—and sometimes the only place—for a black man to exercise leadership and responsibility" (106), he thinks that Woods' energies should be directed toward helping such men achieve their potential instead of stroking his already sizable ego. Instead of building a larger church, Bennett wants to fund scholarships for deserving students, or build a community center for the youth, or even subsidize low-income housing for the poorer members. Bennett wants to help the community. His manhood is tied to his ability to improve the lives of others rather than padding his own personal coffers. Bennett has rejected mainstream (white) society's definition of a successful man (given the circumstances, an unattainable definition) and has embraced a notion of manhood that helps not only him (because it is attainable) but also others in his community.

Abshu, like Bennett, benefits from a decolonized mind and strives to gain for his community political might. Unlike the self-centered Woods, Abshu, unfazed by the insignificant gewgaws of material wealth, wants simply to serve the community. Because of his civic commitment Abshu rallied the community to support Woods in his bid for a council seat, thinking that if Brewster Place had African-American representation, it might finally benefit from the funding that always seemed to elude the neighborhood. But when Woods betrays Brewster Place in his support for its demolition, Abshu, perturbed that Woods has instead supported the white community's agenda, decides that Woods must be removed from office, even though doing so will not alter the outcome for Brewster. At the very least, however, the council will no longer have the sanction of a colonized black mind to justify its actions. Abshu's presence leaves hope that improvements will ultimately be realized for black men and their community. That the novel's epilogue focuses on Abshu is a testament to the potential impact that such a man can have on his environment.

Bibliography

NOTE: Page numbers referred to in the text are to the hardcover editions of *Bailey's Cafe* and *The Men of Brewster Place*. For *The Women of Brewster Place, Linden Hills*, and *Mama Day*, the page references are to the paperback editions.

WORKS BY GLORIA NAYLOR

Novels

The Women of Brewster Place. New York: Viking, 1982. Rpt. New York: Penguin, 1983.
Linden Hills. New York: Ticknor & Fields, 1985. Rpt. New York: Penguin, 1986.
Mama Day. New York: Ticknor & Fields, 1988. Rpt. New York: Vintage, 1989.
Bailey's Cafe. New York: Harcourt, 1992. Rpt. New York: Vintage, 1993.
The Men of Brewster Place. New York: Hyperion, 1998. Rpt. New York: Hyperion Trade, 1999.

Other Works

Bailey's Cafe. (play; April 1994). Hartford Stage Company.
Editor, *Children of the Night: The Best Short Stories by Black Writers, 1967 to the Present*. Boston: Little, Brown, 1996.
"Eva McKinney—A Life of Toil, A Triumph of Spirit: Reminiscences of the Old South." *People* (March 11, 1985): 86–88.
"Finding Our Voice." *Essence* (May 1995): 193.

"Graceful Passages." *Essence* (May 1991): 136.

"Hers." *New York Times* (January 30, 1986): C2 (writing on *Wheel of Fortune*).

"Hers." *New York Times* (February 6, 1986): C2 (on dating for African-American women).

"Hers." *New York Times* (February 13, 1986): C2 (on psychic phenomena).

"Hers." *New York Times* (February 20, 1986): C2 (on the power of the spoken word).

"Hers." *New York Times Magazine* (December 20, 1992): 14 (on the holiday season).

"Love and Sex in the Afro-American Novel." *Yale Review* 78 (Autumn 1988): 19–31.

"The Love of Books." In *The Writing Life*. Eds. Neil Baldwin and Diane Osen. New York: Random House, 1995. 167–75.

"A Message to Winston: To Black Men Who Are Gay." *Essence* (November 1982): 79–85.

"Myth of the Matriarch." *Life* (Spring 1988): 65.

"Reflections." *Centennial*. Ed. Michael Rosenthal. New York: Pindar Press, 1986. 68–71.

"Telling Tales and Mississippi Sunsets." *Grand Mothers: Poems, Reminiscences, and Short Stories About the Keepers of Our Traditions*. Ed. Nikki Giovanni. New York: Holt, 1994. 59–62.

"Until Death Do Us Part." *Essence* (May 1985): 133.

"The Women of Brewster Place." (consultant for television movie, 1988).

INTERVIEWS

Carroll, Rebecca, ed. "Gloria Naylor." *I Know What the Red Clay Looks Like: The Voice and Vision of Black Women Writers*. New York: Crown, 1994. 158–73.

"A Conversation with Gloria Naylor." *Essence* (June 1998): 70.

Cleage, Pearl. "Gloria Naylor." *Catalyst* (Summer 1988): 56–59.

Denison, D. C. "Gloria Naylor." *Boston Globe Magazine* (February 13, 1994): 7.

Denison, D. C. "Interview with Gloria Naylor." *The Writer* (December 1994): 21.

Doten, Patti. "Naylor in Her Glory." *Boston Globe* (October 21, 1992): 77.

Epel, Naomi, ed. "Gloria Naylor." *Writers Dreaming*. New York: Carol Southern Books, 1993. 167–77.

Gloch, Allison. "A Woman to Be Reckoned With." *Special Report* (January–February 1993): 22–25.

Goldstein, William. "A Talk with Gloria Naylor." *Publishers Weekly* 224 (September 9, 1983): 35–36.

Naylor, Gloria, and Toni Morrison. "A Conversation." *Southern Review* 21 (July 1985): 567–93.

Pate, Willard, ed. "Do You Think of Yourself as a Woman Writer?" *Furman Studies* 34 (December 1988): 2–13.

Pearlman, Mickey. "An Interview with Gloria Naylor." *High Plains Literary Review* 5 (Spring 1990): 98–107.

Pearlman, Mickey, and Katherine Usher Henderson. "Gloria Naylor." *Inter/View: Talks with America's Writing Women.* Lexington: University Press of Kentucky, 1990. 23–29.

Perry, Donna, ed. "Gloria Naylor." *Backtalk: Women Writers Speak Out.* New Brunswick: Rutgers University Press, 1993. 215–44.

Rowell, Charles. "An Interview with Gloria Naylor." *Callaloo* 20 (1997): 179–92.

Trescott, Jacqueline. "The Painful Salvation of Gloria Naylor." *Washington Post* (October 21, 1983): D1, 4.

Wilson, Charles E., Jr. "Interview with Gloria Naylor." Conducted via telephone from Virginia Beach, VA, to Brooklyn, NY. August 25, 2000.

"The Woman Behind *The Women of Brewster Place.*" *Ebony* (March 1989): 126.

BIOGRAPHICAL INFORMATION

"Gloria Naylor." *Call & Response: The Riverside Anthology of the African American Literary Tradition.* Ed. Patricia Liggins Hill. New York: Houghton Mifflin, 1998. 1835–37.

"Gloria Naylor." *Contemporary African American Novelists: A Bio-Bibliographical Critical Sourcebook.* Eds. Sarah Wheliss and Emmanuel S. Nelson. Westport, CT: Greenwood Press, 1999. 366–76.

"Gloria Naylor." *Norton Anthology of African American Literature.* Eds. Henry Louis Gates, Jr., and Nellie Y. McKay. New York: Norton, 1997. 2542–43.

"Gloria Naylor." *World Authors, 1980–1985.* Ed. Vineta Colby. New York: H. W. Wilson, 1991. 636–38.

Haralson, Eric L. "Gloria Naylor." *African American Writers.* Ed. Valerie Smith. New York: Scribner's, 1991. 335–46.

Hubbard, Dolan. "Gloria Naylor." *The Oxford Companion to Women's Writing in the United States.* Eds. Cathy N. Davidson and Linda Wagner-Martin. New York: Oxford University Press, 1995. 622–23.

Lewis, Vashti Crutcher. "Gloria Naylor." *Dictionary of Literary Biography.* Vol. 173. Detroit: Gale Research, 1996. 170–76.

Yohe, Kristine A. "Gloria Naylor." *The Oxford Companion to African American Literature.* Eds. William L. Andrews, Frances Smith Foster, and Trudier Harris. New York: Oxford University Press, 1997. 527–29.

REVIEWS

The Women of Brewster Place

Christian Science Monitor, August 12, 1983: B4.

Freedomways 23 (1983): 282–85.

Journal of Black Studies 14 (1984): 389–90.
Library Journal, June 15, 1982: 1242.
London Times, April 21, 1983.
New Republic, September 6, 1982: 37–38.
New York Times Book Review, August 22, 1982: 11, 25.
Washington Post, August 13, 1982: D2.

Linden Hills

Callaloo 8 (1985): 484–88.
Christian Science Monitor, March 1, 1985: B1.
Commonweal, May 3, 1985: 283–85.
Crisis 92 (1985): 13, 47–48.
Freedomways 25 (1985): 227.
Library Journal, April 15, 1985: 86.
London Review of Books, August 1, 1985: 26.
Ms., June 1985: 69–71.
New York Times Book Review, March 3, 1985: 11.
Publishers Weekly, February 14, 1986.
Times Literary Supplement, May 24, 1985: 572.
Washington Post Book World, March 24, 1985: 7.
Women's Review of Books, August 1985: 7–8.

Mama Day

Christian Century, November 16, 1988: 1047–48.
Christian Science Monitor, February 5, 1988: B1–2.
Essence, July 1988: 28.
Kirkus Review, December 15, 1987: 1695.
Library Journal, February 15, 1988: 179.
Ms., February 1988: 74.
New York Times Book Review, February 21, 1988: 7.
North Dakota Quarterly 57 (1989): 176.
Publishers Weekly, December 18, 1987.
SAGE 6 (1989): 56–57.
Southern Review 24 (1988): 680–85.
Times Literary Supplement, June 3, 1988: 623.
Village Voice, March 15, 1988: 52.
Washington Post Book World, February 28, 1988: 5.

Bailey's Cafe

America, February 13, 1993: 17–18.
Atlanta Journal Constitution, September 6, 1992: K8.

Book World, October 11, 1992: 5.

Boston Globe, October 21, 1992: F77.

Chicago Tribune, October 4, 1992: sec. 14, p. 6.

Detroit News & Free Press, September 20, 1992: F7.

Ebony, December 1992: 18.

Guardian, July 30, 1992: B27.

Kenyon Review, 15 (1993): 197.

Kirkus Review, June 15, 1992.

Library Journal, September 1, 1992: 215.

Los Angeles Times Book Review, September 27, 1992: 14.

New York Times Book Review, October 4, 1992: 11–12.

Obsidian II 8 (1993): 111–15.

Publishers Weekly, June 15, 1992.

San Francisco Chronicle Book Review, September 20, 1992: 1.

St. Louis Post-Dispatch, October 25, 1992: C5.

Times Literary Supplement, July 17, 1992: 20.

Times-Picayune, October 18, 1992: E9.

USA Today, November 5, 1992: D4.

Washington Post Book Review, October 11, 1992: 5.

Washington Times, August 30, 1992: B8.

Women's Review of Books, February 1993: 15–16.

The Men of Brewster Place

Advocate, April 14, 1998: 73.

African American Review 33 (1999): 543–45.

African American Review 34 (2000): 176–77.

Afro-American, April 24, 1999: B7.

Atlanta Journal Constitution, January 18, 1998: K7.

Black Issues in Higher Education, December 10, 1998.

Boston Globe, April 26, 1998: L3.

Chicago Defender, May 5, 1998: sec. 2, p. 11.

Chicago Tribune, May 24, 1998: sec. 14, p. 6.

Denver Post, April 26, 1998: E4.

Ebony, May 1998: 14.

Essence, June 1998: 70.

Florida Times Union, July 12, 1998: H4.

Houston Chronicle, June 9, 1998: D1.

Los Angeles Times Book Review, April 26, 1998: 13.

New York Times Book Review, April 19, 1998: 19.

Oral History Review 26 (1999): 173–75.

People, June 22, 1998: 39.

Publishers Weekly, February 23, 1998.

Seattle Times, June 2, 1998: E1.

St. Louis Post-Dispatch, July 3, 1998: E7.
Washington Post, May 8, 1998: F2.

CRITICISM

Andrews, Larry R. "Black Sisterhood in Gloria Naylor's Novels." *CLA Journal* 33 (Fall 1989): 1–25.

Christian, Barbara. "Gloria Naylor's Geography: Community, Class, and Patriarchy in *The Women of Brewster Place* and *Linden Hills.*" In *Reading Black, Reading Feminist: A Critical Anthology.* Ed. Henry Louis Gates, Jr. New York: Penguin, 1990. 348–73.

Collins, G. Michelle. "There Where We Are Not: The Magical Real in *Beloved* and *Mama Day.*" *Southern Review* 24 (1988): 680–85.

Erickson, Peter. "Shakespeare's Naylor, Naylor's Shakespeare: Shakespearean Allusion As Appropriation in Gloria Naylor's Quartet." In *Literary Influence and African American Writers.* Ed. Tracy Mishkin. New York: Garland, 1996. 325–57.

Felton, Sharon, and Michelle C. Loris, eds. *The Critical Response to Gloria Naylor.* Westport, CT: Greenwood Press, 1997.

Fowler, Virginia C. *Gloria Naylor: In Search of Sanctuary.* New York: Twayne, 1996.

Gates, Henry Louis, Jr. and K. Anthony Appiah, eds. *Gloria Naylor: Critical Perspectives Past and Present.* New York: Amistad, 1993.

"Gloria Naylor." *Black Literature Criticism*, Vol. 3, edited by James Draper. Detroit: Gale Research, 1992. 1482–94.

"Gloria Naylor." *Contemporary Literary Criticism*, Vol. 52, edited by Daniel Marowski and Roger Matuz. Detroit: Gale Research, 1989. 319–27.

Harris, Trudier. *The Power of the Porch: The Storyteller's Craft in Zora Neale Hurston, Gloria Naylor, and Randall Kenan.* Athens: University of Georgia Press, 1996.

Kelley, Margot Anne. *Gloria Naylor's Early Novels.* Gainesville, University Press of Florida, 1999.

Kubitchek, Missy Dehn. "Toward a New Order: Shakespeare, Morrison, and Gloria Naylor's *Mama Day.*" *MELUS* 19 (Fall 1994): 75–90.

Meisenhelder, Susan. " 'Eating Cane' in Gloria Naylor's *The Women of Brewster Place* and Zora Neale Hurston's 'Sweat.' " *Notes on Contemporary Literature* 23 (1993): 5–7.

Puhr, Kathleen M. "Healers in Gloria Naylor's Fiction." *Twentieth Century Literature* 40 (1994): 518–27.

Stave, Shirley A. *Gloria Naylor: Strategy and Technique, Magic and Myth.* Newark: University of Delaware Press, 2000.

Storhoff, Gary. " 'The Only Voice Is Your Own': Gloria Naylor's Revision of *The Tempest.*"*African American Review* 29 (Spring 1995): 35–45.

Tanner, Laura E. "Reading Rape: Sanctuary and *The Women of Brewster Place.*" *American Literature* 62 (1990): 559–82.

Thompson, Dorothy Perry. "Gloria Naylor's *Mama Day* and the New Renaissance: Zora As Mother." *Postscript* 13 (1996): 33–45.

Traub, Valerie. "Rainbows of Darkness: Deconstructing Shakespeare in the Work of Gloria Naylor and Zora Neale Hurston." In *Cross-Cultural Performances: Differences in Women's Re-Visions of Shakespeare.* Ed. Marianne Novy. Urbana: University of Illinois Press, 1993. 150–64.

Ward, Catherine C. "Gloria Naylor's *Linden Hills*: A Modern Inferno." *Contemporary Literature* 28 (1987): 67–81.

Warren, Nagueyalti. "Cocoa and George: A Love Dialectic." *SAGE: A Scholarly Journal on Black Women* 7 (1990): 19–25.

Whitt, Margaret Earley. *Understanding Gloria Naylor.* Columbia: University of South Carolina Press, 1999.

Wilson, Charles E., Jr. "Medievalism, Race, and Social Order in Gloria Naylor's *Bailey's Cafe.*" *Studies in Medievalism* 10 (1998): 74–91.

WORKS OF GENERAL INTEREST

Andrews, William, Frances Smith Foster, and Trudier Harris, eds. *The Oxford Companion to African American Literature.* New York: Oxford University Press, 1997.

Barry, Peter. *Beginning Theory: An Introduction to Literary and Cultural Theory.* Manchester, England: Manchester University Press, 1995.

Chaucer, Geoffrey. *The Canterbury Tales.* In *The Complete Poetry and Prose of Geoffrey Chaucer.* Ed. John H. Fisher. New York: Holt, 1977.

Christian, Barbara. *Black Feminist Criticism: Perspectives on Black Women Writers.* New York: Pergamon Press, 1985.

Collins, Patricia Hill. *Black Feminist Thought.* New York: Routledge, 1991.

Dante Alighieri. *The Divine Comedy.* New York: Random House, 1986.

Douglass, Frederick. *Narrative of the Life of Frederick Douglass.* 1845. New York: Signet, 1997.

DuBois, W. E. B. *The Souls of Black Folk.* 1903. Rpt. New York: Penguin, 1996.

Ellison, Ralph. *Invisible Man.* 1952. Rpt. New York: Vintage, 1989.

Equiano, Olaudah. *The Interesting Narrative and Other Writings.* Ed. Vincent Carretta. New York: Penguin, 1995.

Gaines, Ernest J. *A Lesson Before Dying.* New York: Knopf, 1993.

Gates, Henry Louis, Jr., ed. *Reading Black, Reading Feminist: A Critical Anthology.* New York: Penguin, 1990.

Gates, Henry Louis, Jr., and Nellie McKay, eds. *The Norton Anthology of African American Literature.* New York: Norton, 1997.

Hill, Patricia Liggins, ed. *Call & Response: The Riverside Anthology of the African American Literary Tradition.* New York: Houghton Mifflin, 1998.

Holloway, Karla F. C. *The Apocalypse in African American Fiction.* Gainesville: University Press of Florida, 1996.

————. *Moorings and Metaphors: Figures of Culture and Gender in Black Women's Literature*. New Brunswick: Rutgers University Press, 1992.

Huggins, Nathan Irvin. *Harlem Renaissance*. New York: Oxford University Press, 1971.

Hughes, Langston. "The Negro Artist and the Racial Mountain." 1926. Rpt. *The Norton Anthology of African American Literature*. Eds. Henry Louis Gates, Jr., and Nellie Y. McKay. New York: Norton, 1997. 1267–71.

Hurston, Zora Neale. "Sweat." 1926. Rpt. *Spunk: The Selected Short Stories of Zora Neale Hurston*. Berkeley: Turtle Island Foundation, 1985. 38–53.

————. *Their Eyes Were Watching God*. 1937. New York: Harper Collins, 1990.

Jacobs, Harriet. *Incidents in the Life of a Slave Girl*. 1861. Cambridge: Harvard University Press, 1987.

Kubitschek, Missy Dehn. *Claiming the Heritage: African American Women Novelists and History*. Jackson: University Press of Mississippi, 1991.

Locke, Alain, ed. *The New Negro*. 1925. New York: Atheneum, 1968.

Lynn, Steven. *Texts and Contexts: Writing About Literature with Critical Theory*. 2nd edition. New York: Addison-Wesley, 1998.

Morrison, Toni. *The Bluest Eye*. New York: Knopf, 1970. Rpt. New York: Simon and Schuster, 1972.

————. *Beloved*. New York: Knopf, 1987.

————. *Paradise*. New York: Knopf, 1998.

————. *Song of Solomon*. New York: Knopf, 1977. Rpt. New York: Penguin, 1987.

————. *Sula*. New York: Knopf, 1973. Rpt. New York: Penguin, 1982.

Shakespeare, William. *The Tempest*. In *The Riverside Shakespeare*. Eds. G. Blakemore Evans and J. J. M. Tobin. Boston: Houghton Mifflin, 1997.

Walker, Alice. *The Color Purple*. 1982. New York: Washington Square Press, 1998.

————. *In Search of Our Mother's Gardens: Womanist Prose by Alice Walker*. New York: Harcourt, 1983.

Washington, Booker T. *Up from Slavery*. 1901. Rpt. New York: Signet, 2000.

West, Cornel. "Teaching the History of the Civil Rights Movement, 1865–1965." Lecture at Summer Institute of the National Endowment for the Humanities. Harvard University. June 26, 1998.

Willis, Susan. *Specifying: Black Women Writing the American Experience*. Madison: University of Wisconsin Press, 1987.

Wright, Richard. "Blueprint for Negro Writing." 1937. Rpt. *The Norton Anthology of African American Literature*. Eds. Henry Louis Gates, Jr., and Nellie Y. McKay. New York: Norton, 1997. 1380–88.

————. *Native Son*. 1940. Rpt. New York: Harper, 1989.

Index

About the Author

CHARLES E. WILSON, Jr., is Associate Professor of English at Old Dominion University where he teaches African American Literature, Southern Literature, and American Literature. His previous publications include articles on Gloria Naylor and Ernest J. Gaines.

Critical Companions to Popular Contemporary Writers
Second Series

Rudolfo A. Anaya *by Margarite Fernandez Olmos*

Maya Angelou *by Mary Jane Lupton*

Ray Bradbury *by Robin Anne Reid*

Louise Erdrich *by Lorena L. Stookey*

Ernest J. Gaines *by Karen Carmean*

John Irving *by Josie P. Campbell*

Garrison Keillor *by Marcia Songer*

Jamaica Kincaid *by Lizabeth Paravisini-Gebert*

Barbara Kingsolver *by Mary Jean DeMarr*

Maxine Hong Kingston *by E. D. Huntley*

Terry McMillan *by Paulette Richards*

Larry McMurtry *by John M. Reilly*

Toni Morrison *by Missy Dehn Kubitschek*

Chaim Potok *by Sanford Sternlicht*

Amy Tan *by E. D. Huntley*

Anne Tyler *by Paul Bail*

Leon Uris *by Kathleen Shine Cain*

Critical Companions to Popular Contemporary Writers
First Series—*also available on CD-ROM*